Minnesota Mediterranean and East European
Monographs

XV

CYPRUS

A Contemporary Problem in Historical Perspective

MINNESOTA MEDITERRANEAN AND EAST EUROPEAN MONOGRAPHS

Theofanis G. Stavrou, general editor

Minnesota Mediterranean and East European
Monographs

CYPRUS

A Contemporary Problem in Historical Perspective

Van Coufoudakis

MODERN GREEK STUDIES

UNIVERSITY OF MINNESOTA

MINNEAPOLIS, MINNESOTA

Number 15

2006

Minnesota Mediterranean and East European Monographs (MMEEM)

Theofanis G. Stavrou, general editor
Soterios G. Stavrou, associate editor
Elizabeth A. Harry, assistant editor

The objective of the MMEEM is the dissemination of scholarly information about the Mediterranean and East European region. The field is broadly defined to include the social sciences and the humanities. Even though the emphasis of the series is on the Greek and Slavic worlds, there are no thematic, geographical, or chronological limitations. Through the series we hope to encourage research in a variety of contemporary problems in their historical context. In this regard, special efforts will be made to accommodate proceedings from scholarly conferences as well as monographic studies with a diachronic approach.

Monographs in the MMEEM series are published by the Modern Greek Studies Program at the University of Minnesota as supplements to the *Modern Greek Studies Yearbook*. *Cyprus: A Contemporary Problem in Historical Perspective* by Van Coufoudakis is number 15 in the series. Its publication has been made possible by subvention from the Modern Greek Studies Program at the University of Minnesota.

The price for this volume is $30.00, paperback. Make checks payable to:

Modern Greek Studies
325 Social Science Building
UNIVERSITY OF MINNESOTA
267—19th Avenue South
Minneapolis, MN 55455
Telephone: (612) 624-4526

Cover: Watercolor and ink (2006) by Julie Delton

The UNIVERSITY OF MINNESOTA is an equal-opportunity employer.
Printed in the United States of America on acid-free paper

To
The People of Cyprus
My wife Marion
And my daughter Helen

CONTENTS

FOREWORD

A FOREWORD to a good book is at best an intrusion. *Cyprus: A Contemporary Problem in Historical Perspective* is an extraordinarily sensitive and balanced analysis of an international crisis whose most recent phase was created in 1974 when Turkey invaded and occupied 37 percent of the island. Invasion, expulsion, and forcible relocation of peoples, introduction of settlers from mainland Turkey, and a continuous military occupation have truncated the island state which, nevertheless, has managed to survive, demonstrating remarkable political resilience and economic recovery. Still, Nicosia remains the last divided capital of Europe, and Cyprus the only divided member of the European Union. Indeed, according to the author, it was the first state to undergo ethnic cleansing in the period following World War II. As a political scientist, Van Coufoudakis has made the Cyprus Question a lifelong object of study. He has visited the island several times and is as conversant with the various attempts and failures at solution to this question as any living person can be. He certainly has been the most persistent and consistent advocate for a workable solution to the Cyprus Question.

I decided to offer these few remarks because, as general editor of the Minnesota Mediterranean and East European Monographs, I believe that *Cyprus: A Contemporary Problem in Historical Perspective* provides a scholarly assessment which could be useful in the hands of those who honestly seek to understand the nature of the Cyprus Question and those who may strive toward its solution. In some respects the Cyprus Question looks deceptively simple, as it deals with the fate and concerns of a small state with a population of less than one million people. Yet, more than once in the twentieth century, crises in small states lacking political leverage have served as pretexts which led to larger conflicts with wide and grave consequences. Whereas the Cyprus imbroglio affects primarily the various communities living on the island, chief among them the Greek and Turkish Cypriots, its international dimensions involve directly Greece and Turkey and other NATO allies, especially Britain and the United States. Furthermore, now that Cyprus is a member of the European Union, solution to this protracted crisis has become a European concern. As a native Cypriot, brought up in a mixed village of Greek and Turkish Cypriots, I also offer these remarks as testimony of the ability of the two communities to live together, despite the events of the last three decades which have affected the island's political and demographic landscape and the psychological makeup of its people. The latter is especially true of the younger generations of the various communities who have had no appreciable contact, let alone interaction, with each other. Fortunately, during the last two years, interaction has improved. Visits to places of origins are more frequent, and thousands of Turkish Cypriots now residing in the area of Cyprus under military occupation by Turkey are able to seek employment and other benefits in the areas of the republic under government rule.

Since the book at hand is an analysis of a contemporary problem in historical perspective, it is important to keep in mind that the profile of Cyprus, like that of other Mediterranean islands, has been shaped largely by its geographic location. Layers of culture from antiquity to modern times attest to the array of empires and civilizations that left their mark in the process of political, economic, and cultural interaction. Though enriched by such historical experiences, specific cultural identities have survived and indeed flourished. Cyprus has certainly retained its Greek cultural identity, which has always claimed the majority of the island's population. It is also important to keep in mind that historical accidents may play as great a role as imperial designs in the shaping of political culture. Two incidents from the middle of the sixteenth century may serve to illustrate the point. They involve the islands of Malta and Cyprus, located at opposite ends of the Mediterranean, and their respective confrontations with the Ottoman Empire. As is known, the Ottomans attempted to capture Malta in 1565 and failed. In response, Malta under the Knights of the Order of St. John of Jerusalem embarked on a serious undertaking of building or reinforcing massive defensive walls which would serve it well during subsequent centuries. Equally remarkable is the fact that Malta in 1592 was able to found a university. Six years after the abortive attempt to capture Malta, the Ottomans successfully incorporated Cyprus into their realm. The failure of the one imperial venture and the success of the other is a fascinating story in itself, but what is uniquely impressive is the fact that whereas Malta founded its university in 1592, Cyprus did not have a university until 1992, four hundred years later. Multiple reasons may account for this turn of events, one being that empires are not particularly keen on encouraging the establishment of institutions which may incite the ruled to challenge their rulers. The Ottoman Empire held onto Cyprus until 1878 when the island passed to the British, who ruled it until 1960, whereupon, by the Zurich and London Agreements, the island became an independent state in modern times. During the Ottoman period, Cyprus acquired a Turkish community, which at the time of independence stood at 18 percent of the island's population and which had been exploited by the British for political purposes. True, Cyprus did accrue some benefits of modernity from its exposure to British colonial rule. Still, one could argue that the late coming of a university to Cyprus had profound consequences for the island's development. This prolonged xenocratic legacy largely accounts for what has come to be known as the Cyprus Question, and why the latter has never been an entirely Cypriot affair.

In many respects, the Cyprus Question is another chapter in the perennial Eastern Question which, in its diplomatic aspect at least, has to do with the filling of political vacuums created by the weakening or collapse of empires in the region. In the nineteenth century, this vacuum was caused by the gradual decline which led to the collapse of the Ottoman Empire. The process repeated itself in the twentieth century with the reduction of the British Empire

in the eastern Mediterranean. In the twenty-first century, the United States is
the heir of similar imperial ambitions, frustrations, and responsibilities. Developments in the Middle East during the last two decades culminating in the war
in Iraq provide strikingly similar examples of the challenges and responses oc-
casioned by "that shifting, intractable and interwoven tangle of conflicting interests, rival peoples and antagonistic faiths," as the Eastern Question has been
cogently described by John Morley. All of this perhaps explains why, in the
midst of so many Middle Eastern crises, the Cyprus Question has not received
the attention it deserves. Yet, we are repeatedly warned that crises manifested
in this region are interconnected and sooner or later will demand greater attention than they have received thus far.

Even though Coufoudakis places the question in historical perspective,
the strength of his analysis lies in his ability to discuss the latest developments
in various forums where the Cyprus issue is raised. In other words, he treats it
as a current crisis in need of a solution. As a matter of fact, a sizable part of the
book deals with the so-called Annan Plan, which in 2004 was hailed by those
uninformed as a panacea for Cyprus but which in fact proved to be a huge disappointment and was overwhelmingly rejected by the Greek Cypriots, the
largest community of the Republic of Cyprus. It is, indeed, difficult to imagine
how the authors of the plan expected it to be understood and uncritically accepted within a short period of time. Acceptance of the plan would have
amounted to the dissolution of the Republic of Cyprus and the legitimization
of partition, which had been created by the 1974 Turkish invasion. Whatever
the motives and objectives of the Annan Plan, its basic premises were flawed.
Or, as Claire Palley, a distinguished constitutional expert, put it, it was an "international relations debacle." Perhaps this explains the movement which has
been gaining ground and which has been promoting a European solution to the
Cyprus Question, a solution which has as its basic premise the right of the people of Cyprus to have a constitutional convention which will allow them to discuss and determine the kind of constitution by which they should be governed.
This was an opportunity denied the Cypriot people in 1960 when Cyprus became independent. It would have been doubly tragic if an unworkable solution
had been imposed upon them again in 2004.

On the morrow of the failure of the Annan Plan, many well-meaning
observers, who had hoped for a solution to the Cyprus Question, expressed regret that the plan had been rejected. The present book sheds much light on
the reasons for the failure, not only of the Annan Plan but also of other initiatives thus far, and provides the basis on which a workable solution may be con-
structed. The Cyprus Question remains complex and difficult. Sharp disagreements remain part of the discourse between the two major communities
and within the communities themselves. Still, undaunted by the plethora of
difficulties, the government of the Republic of Cyprus continues the search for
a political solution. Perhaps the greatest source of optimism for the future of
the island is the demonstrated political maturity of the Cypriot people and of
its political and cultural elites. Cypriot society and its leaders received little
constructive support when the island gained its independence in 1960 and
when they needed it most. External actors exploited the political good will of
the Greek Cypriots at the time and advocated policies which made the political

experiment of the young, "reluctant republic" truly unworkable. If anything, it was a recipe concocted for failure. Be that as it may, the last forty years have been hard taskmasters for the Cypriots, most of whom have learned their lessons well and are trying to adjust their expectations to the new reality of a culture of peace and prosperity as advocated by the European Union.

During the height of their struggle for independence in the 1950s, the British observer Penelope Tremayne noted that "the Greek Cypriots are a most gentle, friendly . . . intellectual and suppleminded people; not given to violence and bloodshed; not at all suited to it when it comes to the point." This may equally apply to the Turkish Cypriots, at least the Turkish Cypriots of my village whom I knew well. Admittedly, the fate of Cyprus still hangs between the aspirations of the Cypriot people and the mesh of international politics. It is the hope that this volume will contribute toward a clearer understanding of the Cyprus Question, and that its sober analysis will serve those who genuinely seek a solution worthy of the political aspirations of the people of Cyprus.

Theofanis G. Stavrou
University of Minnesota

PREFACE

THE PURPOSE of this book is to bring to the reader basic information about Cyprus and analyze current aspects of what has come to be known as the "Cyprus Problem." I hope that the issues raised, along with the bibliography and the other references, will challenge the reader to explore further the history, culture, and present state of affairs in Aphrodite's island.

This book is not written by a Cypriot. The author has traveled to this beautiful island for more than three decades and has devoted much of his academic career to the study of Cyprus. This is why this book is dedicated to the Cypriot people whose welcome, hospitality, and sacrifices will never be forgotten. The book is also dedicated to my wife Marion and my daughter Helen whose moral support made my work possible. They came to know, appreciate, and love Cyprus as much as I have. I could not ask for more.

I also want to thank my many friends, my colleagues, and various political leaders and diplomats in the United States and Europe who, over the years, willingly gave their time to discuss with me their views on Cyprus. One of them was an exceptional American diplomat, the late Charles W. McCaskill Sr., who served in Cyprus in the first days of the republic. He, too, fell under the spell of this island and its people, without losing his objectivity, good judgment, and integrity.

I extend my appreciation to my respected colleague Theofanis Stavrou for his incisive foreword and to Soterios Stavrou for his editorial assistance. His constructive suggestions helped improve this volume. However, the views expressed and any omissions are exclusively mine.

Public officials and academics have their own informed perspectives of the world and its problems. The wisdom I gained over the years by talking with common people in villages and towns across Cyprus is a testament to their maturity, their integrity, their courage in adversity, and their yearning for peace and coexistence. I wish more foreign diplomats had taken the time to understand this land and its people, rather than attempt to impose schemes serving interests other than those of the people of Cyprus.

CHRONOLOGY

The recorded history of Cyprus dates to the ninth millennium B.C.

Second and first millennia B.C.	Mycenaean and Achaean Greeks settle in Cyprus
30 B.C.– 330 A.D.	Cyprus a province of the Roman Empire
330–1191	Cyprus a province of the Byzantine Empire
1191–1571	Cyprus under the rule of the Crusaders, the Order of the Knights Templar, the French Lusignans (1192–1489), and the Venetians (1489–1571)
1571–1878	Cyprus under Ottoman rule
1878	Cyprus leased by the Ottoman Empire to Britain
1914	Cyprus annexed by Britain following Turkey's alignment with Germany in World War I
1923	Under the Treaty of Lausanne Turkey relinquishes all rights to Cyprus
1925	Cyprus declared a British crown colony
1931	First Greek Cypriot uprising against British rule
1950	Makarios III elected archbishop of Cyprus
1954	Greece brings the issue of self-determination for Cyprus to the UN General Assembly
1955–1959	Greek Cypriot anticolonial struggle

1960	Cyprus granted independence under agreements negotiated in Zurich and London by Greece, Turkey, and Great Britain
16 August	Proclamation of the Republic of Cyprus
1963	President Makarios submits constitutional amendments for discussion which are rejected by the Turkish side Insurrection by Turkish Cypriot extremists
1964	Arrival of UNFICYP (UN peacekeeping force) Turkey bombs and threatens to invade Cyprus; U.S. president Johnson's intervention halts the threatened invasion
1967	Turkey threatens to invade Cyprus; United States (Vance mission) ends the invasion threat
1968	Start of UN-sponsored talks between the Greek and Turkish Cypriot communities to resolve the intercommunal conflict
15 July 1974	Coup against the government of the Republic of Cyprus organized by the military junta of Greece
20 July	Turkey invades Cyprus and occupies nearly 37 percent of the republic
1975	Turkey, through the Turkish Cypriot leadership, declares the "Turkish Federated State of Cyprus" in the areas occupied by the Turkish army
1983	The Turkish Cypriot leadership, with Turkey's support, unilaterally declares the "Turkish Republic of Northern Cyprus" ("TRNC") in the Turkish-occupied areas of the republic; all major international organizations condemn the action, while the UN Security Council declares the secessionist act "legally invalid"
1990	The Republic of Cyprus applies for membership in the EEC
1993	The European Commission issues its positive opinion on the application of Cyprus
1994	The EU Corfu Summit decides that the next phase of enlargement will include Cyprus and Malta The European Court of Justice rules that all direct trade between Turkish-occupied areas of Cyprus and the European Union is illegal

1998	Accession negotiations between Cyprus and the EU commence
November 2001	Turkey threatens to annex the Turkish-occupied areas of Cyprus if the European Union admits the Republic of Cyprus as a full member before a settlement is reached on the Cyprus Question
16 April 2003	The Republic of Cyprus signs the Treaty of Accession to the EU in Athens
23 April	The Turkish occupation regime announces partial lifting of restrictions it imposed in 1974 on the movement of persons across the cease-fire line
24 April 2004	Greek Cypriots overwhelmingly reject the Annan Plan (version V), while Turkish Cypriots, including the settlers, accept it
1 May	The Republic of Cyprus becomes a member of the European Union

CHAPTER ONE

An Introduction to Cyprus

THE REPUBLIC OF CYPRUS gained its independence from Britain on 16 August 1960, following eighty-two years of British colonial rule. Located at the crossroads of civilization and empires, Cyprus, because of its important strategic location, has been affected by the actions of powers that have dominated the Eastern Mediterranean.

The recorded history of the island of Cyprus dates back to 9,000 B.C.[1] Greek culture and civilization was brought to the island by Mycenaean-Achaean Greeks around 1200 B.C. Since then, and despite many conquests, Cyprus has retained its Hellenic character and culture. The island was under Ottoman control from 1571 until 1878. Ottoman rule permanently altered Cypriot culture, society, and political developments. It introduced a Turkish minority, the Turkish language, and the Islamic faith to an otherwise homogeneous Hellenic and Christian territory. Peaceful bicommunal coexistence marked most of the period of Ottoman and British rule.

In 1974, following a coup against the government of the Republic of Cyprus engineered by the junta ruling Greece at the time, Turkey invaded and occupied nearly 37 percent of the Republic of Cyprus. Today, Cyprus remains the last divided and occupied country of Europe. Thus, the so-called "Cyprus Problem" remains one of invasion, occupation, and violation of the international legal order. Moreover, Turkey's actions constitute a threat to regional stability, especially at a time when Turkey has opened accession negotiations with the European Union. Turkey's actions in Cyprus have been condemned by numerous unanimous UN Security Council resolutions, UN General Assembly resolutions, by decisions of international and domestic courts,[2] and other major regional organizations.

As this book will show, the consequences of invasion and forcible division of the island have resulted in documented violations of human rights, in the massive colonization of the areas under occupation, in the destruction of cultural heritage, ethnic cleansing and separation, and property usurpation. All these actions violate major treaties as well as international and European law which Turkey has ratified over the years.

On 1 May 2004, the Republic of Cyprus joined the European Union. The goal of the island's reunification had not been achieved at the time of EU accession because Turkey favored the imposition of a divisive political solution known as "Annan-V," which was rejected by 76 percent of the Greek Cypriot public in the referendum of 24 April 2004. EU accession, a major goal of successive Cypriot governments, is also an important milestone in the long history of Cyprus that has opened new political, economic, cultural, and social opportunities for all Cypriots. These new opportunities can contribute to the resolution of the Cyprus Question.[3]

This brief book is intended to introduce the reader to basic aspects of the contemporary phase of the Cyprus Question and its historical dimensions. It will identify and analyze turning points in the life of the Republic of Cyprus and also discuss prospects for a viable solution to the Cyprus Question in line with European law, the UN resolutions on Cyprus, international law, and earlier agreements between the leaders of the two communities. Because of its rich history and strategic location, Cyprus has been the subject of many studies[4] from archaeology to diplomacy, from art and literature to economics, politics, and law, and, most recently, studies on ethnic conflict, conflict resolution, and nationalism. Thus, Aphrodite's island has generated a vast and important bibliography not always justified by the small size of the island.

Forces Shaping Modern Cyprus

The focus of this book is on post-independence Cyprus. The island's current political development, however, has been shaped by forces that can be traced to the nineteenth century. The Ottoman conquest of Cyprus (1570–71) permanently altered the culture, the society, the economy, and the political developments on the island. The Turks who settled in Cyprus remained a small minority of the island's population. They ruled the island until 1878, when the British took over the administration of Cyprus as part of their strategic expansion in the Eastern Mediterranean and the Middle East.

The Role of the Orthodox Church

The Ottoman administration in Cyprus was based on the *milliyet* system under which cohesive ethno-religious communities were administered by their respective religious leaders and institutions. The Autocephalous Orthodox Church of Cyprus[5] dates back to the earliest Christian times. Under the *milliyet* system the church was granted secular administrative powers and became the ultimate spokesman of the Greek Cypriot community throughout the years of Ottoman rule. It also became the guardian of Greek culture and heritage on the island. It should be noted that more than 97 percent of the Christian population of Cyprus identified with the Orthodox Church.

The church retained its political and cultural influence during the British colonial administration, despite British attempts to undermine its leadership role.[6] Successive archbishops and bishops of the Church of Cyprus worked closely with the secular leadership and placed church resources in the promotion of *enosis* (the union of Cyprus with Greece), a subject which will be discussed shortly. This was not an unusual role for the Orthodox Church.

Similar was the role of the church during the Ottoman occupation of mainland Greece. Because the church was seen as the guardian of Hellenic culture and heritage in a homogeneous Orthodox Hellenic community, its advocacy of the unionist cause was a natural part of its mission. This was also expected by the public in the absence of other secular political or civil society organizations at the national level. The archbishop of Cyprus became the "ethnarch," the leader of the nation.

The charismatic Archbishop Makarios III became the official spokesman and political leader of the Greek Cypriot unionist movement in the decade of the 1950s. When Cyprus gained its independence in 1960, Makarios became the first popularly elected president of the Republic of Cyprus. He retained this post following several free and competitive elections until his death in 1977. The political involvement of religious leaders may be an alien experience to Western observers whose modern traditions emphasize the separation of church and state. In view of the role of the church in the history and culture of Cyprus and the role of Archbishop Makarios in the liberation struggle that led to the independence of Cyprus, his election to public office was not surprising. During his tenure as president and as archbishop, he kept both roles separate, although each role reinforced the prestige of the other. Since his death in 1977 and the consolidation of the Republic of Cyprus, the church has returned to its traditional religious and cultural role.

Although the church retains significant influence in the daily life of the Greek Cypriot community, its earlier political role has subsided for a number of reasons, including: (1) the development of a vibrant multiparty democratic political system; (2) the rise of civil society organizations; (3) the absence of charismatic church leaders in the tradition of Archbishop/President Makarios; (4) the changing public expectations as to the role of the church in a modern European state; and (5) the church's own understanding of its role in a modern European republic. In post-1974 Cyprus, the church has maintained a consistent position shared with the majority of the Greek Cypriot political leaders and the public on the reunification of the republic. The church remains steadfast against any externally imposed resolution scheme that would formalize and legitimize the results of the 1974 Turkish invasion. The church has been in the forefront of legal actions intended to protect the Greek Cypriot cultural heritage in the Turkish occupied areas of Cyprus.[7] For these reasons, the church as a whole, and individual bishops in particular, took a definitive stand against the plan proposed by UN secretary-general Kofi Annan in March 2004 ("Annan-V"). This plan was rejected by 76 percent of the Greek Cypriot public and by the majority of the secular Greek Cypriot leadership in the 24 April 2004 referendum. This plan and the causes for its rejection by the Greek Cypriots will be discussed later in this volume. In a secular European society, the Autocephalous Orthodox Church of Cyprus remains an important institution in the religious, social, and cultural life of the country.

The Political Development of the Greek Cypriot Community:
The Impact of Colonial Rule

Nineteenth-century Western Europe witnessed the rise of nationalist and unification movements. Similar movements influenced the political development of mainland Greece through the first quarter of the twentieth century, as well as that of the Greek Cypriot community. When the British colonial administration arrived in Cyprus in 1878, it found a defined Greek Cypriot nationalist movement seeking the union of Cyprus to Greece. The Greek Cypriot unionist movement reflected the view commonly held in Greek-inhabited lands of the Eastern Mediterranean, Anatolia, and the Balkans that they were a natural part of Hellenism and that time had arrived for the union of such territories to the newly independent Greek kingdom. After the transfer of authority to Great Britain, Greek Cypriot political aspirations were affected by Britain's regional strategic interests and reliance on divide-and-rule policies among the two communities in order to defuse Greek Cypriot political demands. Separatist policies were the hallmark of British colonial administration in Cyprus. These policies were rationalized in terms of protecting the interests of the Turkish Cypriot minority.[8]

Greek Cypriot political frustrations increased even more because of Britain's unwillingness to provide for self-government on the island recognizing majoritarian and democratic principles. Britain also failed to bring about economic reform and development on the island. These factors contributed to two Greek Cypriot uprisings against British rule. The first, in 1931, was easily suppressed by the colonial administration. Britain was unable to control the second Greek Cypriot uprising, which involved both an armed struggle on the island as well as political actions at the United Nations.[9] Because Cyprus was a colonial territory, its case for self-determination was brought to the UN General Assembly by Greece on numerous occasions between 1955 and 1958. In its failed attempt to suppress this uprising, Britain resorted to heavy-handed military tactics, torture, hangings, and other violations of human rights. These violations were brought to the attention of the emerging European human rights institutions. Unfortunately, these cases were withdrawn as part of the overall settlement in 1959 that granted Cyprus its independence. In order to maintain control of Cyprus, Britain also relied on segments of the Turkish Cypriot community which cooperated with the colonial administration.

The Movement for Enosis with Greece

The consequences of Britain's colonial rule were clear. Britain proved unwilling or unable to recognize the seriousness and depth of Greek Cypriot nationalism. It treated each ethnic community as a natural extension of Greece and Turkey. British divide-and-rule policies and its reliance on Turkey and the Turkish Cypriots to neutralize Greek Cypriot political demands increased the communal divide and Greek Cypriot suspicions of Turkey's motives. They also increased Greek Cypriot emotional and political dependence on Greece. This dependence influenced, if not also determined, Greek Cypriot politics both before independence (1930s–1959) and in the first decade and a half of the post-independence period (1960–74). The secular and religious leadership of the Greek Cypriot community could not escape this predicament. All this changed following the 1974 coup against the government of the Republic of Cyprus carried out by the junta ruling Greece at the time. This short-lived coup became the pretext and the rationalization for the 1974 Turkish invasion and subsequent occupation of nearly 37 percent of the republic's territory.

However significant the emotional and actual influence of mainland Greece was on Cypriot politics, society, and culture, influence was a two-way street. The Greek Cypriot community had a long and proud history that evolved both in parallel but also in distinct ways from those of mainland Greece. As an island community, at a significant geographic distance from mainland Greece, Cypriot political, social, cultural, and economic development was different from that of the Greek mainland. Cyprus never experienced the Monarchist/Republican upheavals of the first quarter of the twentieth century, the two world wars, or the civil war that constrained Greek political development. In contrast to Greece, at independence, Cyprus had a flourishing Communist Party, founded in 1923; a powerful church leadership, and a major presence in international fora through its leadership role in the nonaligned movement. President Makarios of Cyprus, with his personal charisma and prestige, could in turn influence Greek politics, except for the period when Greece was under military rule (1967–74).

One unanticipated effect of the tragedy of the Turkish invasion and of the continuing occupation of Cyprus has been that it helped the consolidation and legitimacy of the Republic of Cyprus in the minds of its Greek Cypriot citizens, who constituted 82 percent of the population of the republic. Whatever doubts may have existed about the manner by which the Republic of Cyprus came into being in 1960 have been overcome.[10] The unionist movement, in turn, has faded away in the political history of the island republic. Greek Cypriots are proud of their Hellenic heritage and cognizant of their common interests with Greece, but also recognize that they have independent traditions and separate interests. Over the last century, on numerous occasions, Greece placed its national interests ahead of those of Cyprus, whether in its dealings with the United States, Britain, Turkey, or NATO. Greek Cypriots have accepted this bitter reality. The Republic of Cyprus and its political leadership now perceive their relationship to Greece as one of equals and not, any longer, as one of dependence on the "national center of Hellenism," i.e. Greece. After 1974, Greece has also come to respect and accept this reality.

Until independence in 1960, national level politics were virtually absent from Cyprus. Power was concentrated in the hands of the British colonial administration. In the pre-independence period, Greek Cypriot political activity at the national level focused on the quest for self-determination and union with Greece, and on the degree of cooperation, or lack thereof, with the colonial authorities. Most political activity concentrated on municipal contests. The first major national political party in Cyprus that attracted members from both Cypriot communities was the Communist Party of Cyprus which was founded in 1923.[11] In 1925, the party evolved into the Progressive Party of the Working People (AKEL), which remains to this day the largest and best organized Greek Cypriot political party. The church, along with the Greek Cypriot middle and upper classes, channeled their political activities through smaller conservative parties.

The externally imposed independence constitution, with its divisive electoral procedures and institutions, gave rise to a communally based pluralist political party system representing a broad ideological spectrum. Until his death in 1977, Makarios, the charismatic archbishop and president of the Republic of Cyprus, was also the great conciliator among the diverse Greek Cypriot political forces. Makarios's charisma and influence may have overshadowed the rise of alternate political leaders, who emerged following his death on 3 August 1977. No one among these leaders has attained Makarios's stature at home or abroad. Today, the Republic of Cyprus is a vibrant democracy with a multiparty system whose influence is felt in all facets of Greek Cypriot political life.

The Political Development of the Turkish Cypriot Community

The British takeover of Cyprus in 1878 transformed the status of the Turkish Cypriots from that of the ruling class to a minority under foreign rule. The 1923 Lausanne Treaty formally ended World War I in the region and settled all outstanding territorial issues. The new Turkish Republic under Kemal Ataturk renounced its claims on Cyprus.

The economic, social, cultural, and political development of the Turkish Cypriots lagged behind that of the Greek Cypriot community. Turkish Cypriot political consciousness grew slowly through the first quarter of the twentieth century. It often developed in response to the dynamism of the Greek Cypriot enosis movement and to the manipulation of the British colonial authorities. During the interwar period, Turkish Cypriots perceived Britain as the protector of their rights, remained loyal to the Crown, and opposed Greek Cypriot calls for self-determination and union with Greece. In turn, the British colonial authorities came to depend on the Turkish Cypriot minority to defuse Greek Cypriot political demands.

By the early 1950s, Britain encouraged Turkey to revive its claims on Cyprus. This was intended to secure Turkey's cooperation in Britain's Middle East security schemes and to blunt Greek and Greek Cypriot demands for self-determination on the island. Britain also encouraged the formation of the Turk Mukavemet Teskilati (Turkish Resistance Organization, or TMT), a Turkish Cypriot armed militant organization to counter the Greek Cypriot anticolonial uprising (1955–59). A Turkish Cypriot conservative leader, Dr. Fazil Kutchuk, formed in 1955 the Cyprus Turkish National Union, a political party designed to promote Turkish Cypriot political claims. Upon independence in 1960, Kutchuk became the first elected vice president of the Republic of Cyprus. The conservative domination of the Turkish Cypriot political scene effectively neutralized any action along class or communal lines. Moreover, intercommunal political activity was discouraged by the divisive provisions of the externally imposed 1960 constitution. A small number of Turkish Cypriots who cooperated with the left-wing Greek Cypriot AKEL party faced intimidation and violence in their own community.

In December 1963 following problems in the implementation of the 1960 constitution, the Turkish Cypriots withdrew from their positions in the government. Since then, they have challenged the legality of the internationally recognized government of the Republic of Cyprus. In the aftermath of the 1974 Turkish invasion, they also challenged the legitimacy of the internationally recognized Republic of Cyprus, not just merely that of its government. Ironically, since the 2003 lifting by the Turkish authorities of some of the restrictions on movement across the cease-fire line, Turkish Cypriots have massively sought identity cards, passports, and other documents issued by the Republic of Cyprus, the very republic that their leadership has been trying to repudiate.

The period from December 1963 to July 1974 was marked by intermittent communal violence and threats of a Turkish military intervention. Talks were also held by the two communities, under UN auspices, for revisions to the 1960 constitution. A near agreement on a revised constitution had been reached by the summer of 1974. This agreement was destroyed by the short-lived coup staged in Nicosia against the government of Cyprus by the junta ruling Greece at the time. Using that as an opportunity and a pretext, Turkey invaded Cyprus on 20 July 1974. Since then, it has continued to occupy nearly 37 percent of the Republic of Cyprus.

The Turkish Cypriots and Turkey

Turkish Cypriot dependence on Turkey increased following the intercommunal incidents that commenced in December 1963. There were additional consequences as well. Kutchuk, the more moderate Turkish Cypriot political leader and vice president of the republic, was soon sidelined by Rauf Denktash, a British-educated attorney and president of the Turkish Cypriot communal chamber. Thereafter, Denktash dominated the Turkish Cypriot political scene for nearly four decades. A Turkish nationalist, Denktash was elected president of the so-called "Turkish Federated State of Cyprus," an unrecognized entity created in 1975 in areas occupied by the Turkish military. Following the 1983 unilateral declaration of independence of the areas of the Republic of Cyprus under Turkish occupation, Denktash became president of the so-called "Turkish Republic of Northern Cyprus" (TRNC). Only Turkey recognizes this illegal entity and its proclaimed president.

Despite the rise of several small Turkish Cypriot political parties in the occupied areas, Denktash maintained his power through a combination of charisma, manipulation, intimidation by extremist organizations such as the TMT and the Grey Wolves, and the support of the Turkish occupation army. In contrast to the maturing relationship between Greece and the Republic of Cyprus, Turkey has consolidated its influence and control over Turkish Cypriot political life. A number of factors explain this dependent relationship, including: (1) the economic dependence of the occupied areas on Turkey; (2) the implantation of settlers from mainland Turkey who now outnumber the native Turkish Cypriot population; and (3) the presence of more than 40,000 heavily armed Turkish occupation troops whose commanders control political developments of the occupied areas.

Rauf Denktash has been the only Turkish Cypriot leader who was able to exert certain degree of political influence in Ankara. This was due to the coincidence of his vision of Cyprus with that of the Turkish military. In view of the power structure in Ankara, Denktash could count on the military to counter any policies of Turkish civilian governments that may have been different from his. By 2003, Denktash's manipulative powers were curbed by a regime change engineered in the occupied areas by Turkish prime minister Recep Tayyip Erdogan with the connivance of the Turkish military. Denktash was eventually replaced by Mehmet Ali Talat, another Turkish Cypriot politician, whose "moderate" image fits Erdogan's and the military's European mission. Talat's rise to power in occupied Nicosia signals the rise of Ankara's influence in the occupied areas and Talat's total dependence on Ankara's Cypriot policy. This is because Talat never developed political connections in Ankara similar to those of Denktash.

Islam and the Turkish Cypriots

The role of religion in the Turkish Cypriot community needs to be discussed in the context of the minority community's political development. The secularization of the Turkish Republic in 1923 under Kemal Ataturk affected the cultural and religious development of the Turkish Cypriot community as well. Turkish Cypriot secularism was strengthened by the impact of Ataturk's reforms and the policies of the British colonial administration. The Sunni Muslim traditions and practices were part of the Turkish Cypriot culture but did not control the daily life of the average Turkish Cypriot urban dweller as Islam did in other parts of the Middle East.

Since the 1974 Turkish invasion of Cyprus there has been a distinct revival of Sunni Islam in the occupied areas. Driving through the occupied areas today, one is struck not only by the plundering of Orthodox churches, but also by the massive building of new mosques in urban and rural areas. A number of reasons account for this development: (1) the dominant presence of Anatolian settlers who were not affected as much by Ataturk's forced secularization; (2) the greater tolerance of Islam by the current leadership in Ankara; and (3) the internal political dynamics of the Turkish Cypriot community.

In an attempt to solicit political support, economic assistance, and investments from Saudi Arabia, Denktash ended up encouraging the revival of religion in the occupied areas. Denktash used religion in his construction of a new Turkish Cypriot identity and foreign policy as he went about the creation of the new "state" in the occupied areas. One is struck by the frequent references in Denktash's post-1976 speeches about "the Turkish Cypriot Muslim people." This was absent from the earlier political discourse. In this manner, Denktash attempted to place the Turkish Cypriots in the context of a broader Islamic world. It also helped him in his campaign to obtain political support and recognition by other Islamic countries. In the process, Denktash sought to join the Organization of Islamic Countries. But the Turkish Cypriots have only managed to secure an observer status in that organization as a community and not as a state. The future of the Islamic revival in occupied Cyprus will have to be watched closely, as it will affect political developments in and around Cyprus, as well as the attitude of the Turkish military guardians of occupied Cyprus.

Conclusion

The preceding analysis shows that because of circumstances largely external to Cyprus, the two communities followed separate political development paths. However, with minor exceptions, the two communities coexisted peacefully throughout the island and cooperated in their daily lives. In the aftermath of the Turkish invasion and the ethnic cleansing carried out by the occupation army, the two communities remained largely separated. This lasted until 2003, when the occupation authorities relaxed movement restrictions across the cease-fire line. Greek Cypriots, however, are still denied fundamental rights under European law in the occupied areas.

Following the 1974 Turkish invasion and continuing occupation, Greek Cypriots rallied around the legitimate and internationally recognized Republic of Cyprus, which is now a member of the EU. In the course of UN-sponsored talks for the reunification of the island (1975–2004), the Greek Cypriots have sought a functional and viable solution based on UN Security Council resolutions on Cyprus, European law, and decisions by European and other national courts. In contrast, the Turkish Cypriot leadership, under Turkey's control, has sought to legitimize the separatist and divisive outcome of the 1974 Turkish invasion.

As successive chapters will show, this has been the challenge confronting international interlocutors who have offered their services under the mission of "good offices" of the UN secretary-general. Their task has been complicated further by the involvement of parties external to Cyprus whose regional strategic interests have little to do with the search for a viable and functional solution that would reunify Cyprus and its people within the context of the EU.

This book, however, will end on an optimistic note. The Republic of Cyprus, as a member of the EU, is now a part of a wider European community of sovereign and territorially integral states where human rights, diversity, and regionalism are respected and protected. It is in this context that the unity as well as the diversity of the Republic of Cyprus can be advanced and secured for the benefit of all Cypriots.

CHAPTER TWO

Cyprus Today

THIS CHAPTER identifies and analyzes the contemporary dimensions of the Cyprus Question. It explores the causes of the lack of a political settlement, despite decades of negotiations and continuous concessions by successive Cypriot governments. The analysis identifies key issues in dispute among the parties involved. The chapter will conclude with a discussion of Turkey's EU accession negotiations and how these negotiations affect and reflect the contemporary dimensions of the Cyprus Question.

The Nature of the Political Question

On 1 May 2004 the internationally recognized Republic of Cyprus became a member of the European Union (EU). Even though an EU member, Cyprus remains the last divided and occupied country of Europe as a result of the 1974 Turkish invasion and continuing occupation. Consequently, the *acquis communautaire* (the body of legislation guiding European Union policy) is applied only in the free areas of the republic. The "Cyprus Problem," as it is commonly referred to in international political analyses and journalistic accounts, remains one of invasion and occupation, an affront to the post-Cold War international legal and political order, and a threat to regional stability.

Despite the condemnation of Turkey's actions by unanimous UN Security Council resolutions, international and domestic court decisions, General Assembly resolutions, and resolutions by various other regional organizations, the Cyprus Question remains unresolved.[1] This and the next chapter explore the reasons for this deadlock, which undermines the credibility of international institutions and the international political and legal order. The plight of a small and weak country that has been forcibly divided and occupied must be addressed soon. A resolution conforming to international law, UN Security Council resolutions, international and domestic court decisions, European law, and the high-level agreements between the leaders of the two communities (1977 and 1979) is the only way to protect the rights of all citizens of the Republic of Cyprus regardless of ethnicity or religion. Such a solution is long overdue.

Addressing the sixtieth session of the UN General Assembly on 18 September 2005, President Tassos Papadopoulos of Cyprus reiterated his country's readiness to seek a resolution of the Cyprus Question under the UN secretary-general's mission of good offices so as to bring about the reunification of the country, its society, economy, and institutions. President Papadopoulos specifically called for a sustained negotiation process that:

- would facilitate a negotiated settlement without any arbitration on the part of the secretary-general or his emissaries. This position can be explained by the fact that under the American- and British-sponsored UN negotiating initiative (February–March 2004), Secretary-General Kofi Annan unilaterally assumed arbitration powers as a condition of his engagement in the search for a solution to the Cyprus Question. This led to his formulation of a 10,000-page-long comprehensive plan known as Annan-V, which will be examined in the next chapter. This plan was rejected in a referendum held on 24 April 2004 by 76 percent of the Greek Cypriot public for reasons that will be discussed later.
- would involve the active contribution of the European Union in the negotiation process. This provision reflected the negotiating experience of February–March 2004. Under U.S., British, and Turkish pressure, Secretary-General Annan relegated the EU to an observer status only, instead of an active participant in the negotiation process. Consequently, most of the provisions of Annan-V, the comprehensive arbitration plan produced by the secretary-general's staff, did not conform to European law or to European court decisions on Cyprus. These derogations from European law would have made all Cypriot citizens second-class citizens in the EU. These derogations would be justified because they would have entered into force under a bicommunal agreement, approved by a referendum, prior to the accession of the Republic of Cyprus to the EU.
- only an agreed settlement endorsed by the leadership of the two communities would be put to a referendum. This also reflected the experience of the 2004 round of negotiations. Annan-V, the plan that was presented for approval at the 24 April 2004 referenda of the two communities, was not the product of negotiations but of the secretary-general's arbitration.
- there would be no deadlines in the negotiation process dictated by exogenous elements. This provision also reflected the 2004 experience. As a precondition for his involvement in the talks, Annan, early in February 2004, set rigid deadlines for the parties to reach an agreement. Each step of the negotiation was to be completed by set dates between the middle of February and the end of March 2004. On 24 April 2004 the two communities, in separate and simultaneous referenda, were to accept or reject the comprehensive plan. The reasons for the rigid schedule were clear. The plan proposed by the secretary-general, with the support and participation of the United States and Britain, would replace the Republic of Cyprus with a new confederation of two largely autonomous states. The plan also contained

serious derogations from the *acquis communautaire*. This is why the secretary-general's plan had to be accepted prior to 1 May 2004, so that the new political entity would accede to the EU instead of the internationally recognized Republic of Cyprus.

- would bring about a settlement reflecting the concerns and expectations of the people of Cyprus and not the interests of foreign powers on the island. This provision responded to British and Turkish attempts to introduce provisions in the UN comprehensive plan that had nothing to do with the constitutional settlement on Cyprus. For example, Britain attempted to expand its rights in the sovereign base areas it maintains on Cypriot soil. These bases were part of the agreements that were imposed on Cyprus as a condition of independence in 1960.[2] Turkey, in turn, attempted to introduce provisions in Annan-V annulling the Cypriot accession to the 1936 Montreux Treaty on navigation in the Straits. It also questioned the economic zone agreement between the Republic of Cyprus and Egypt as well as the right of Cyprus to have a continental shelf. Turkey's actions reflected its effort to amend or even annul the 1936 Montreux Treaty, as well as Turkey's positions on continental shelf issues and the Law of the Sea in general.

- would achieve a settlement based on a reunified state without abnormally long transitional periods and not requiring taxing efforts for basic democratic governance. Under Annan-V, a complicated decision-making system was introduced at the national level. Separate voting majorities and minority vetoes were typical. In other key policy areas, unelected and therefore unaccountable representatives of third parties would hold the balance of decision-making power in the new national government. Various integration provisions and Turkish troop withdrawal provisions would be implemented over lengthy time periods with no methods assuring compliance. This is why a functional and workable democratic system is a must.

Finally, the president expressed his hope that Turkey's EU accession process would "radically shift" Turkey's mentality and thus help "rid the Cyprus problem of some of its most intractable components and facilitate a settlement." This statement reflected the hope that Turkey's intransigence over Cyprus would be moderated as Turkey proceeded with its accession talks with the EU. Turkey's occupation of the territory of an EU country member, and the continuing violations of the rights of all Cypriot citizens by Turkish occupation forces, had to be addressed if Turkey aspired to become an EU member. Membership of the Republic of Cyprus in the EU could give a new impetus for the protection of human rights for all Cypriots through European institutions and procedures. This had always been a major stumbling bloc in the negotiations prior to the accession of Cyprus in the EU. For these and other reasons the Republic of Cyprus supported the EU decision to grant a date for the commencement of accession talks with Turkey. Unfortunately, Turkey has yet to reciprocate. At the time of this writing, Turkey continues to refuse to recognize the Republic of Cyprus, one of the twenty-five EU members that will have to agree to Turkey's eventual accession to the EU. In addition, Turkey's ports, airports, and air corridors remain closed to Cypriot shipping and aircraft, in violation of the EU/Turkey Customs Union Agreement.[3]

Brief addresses by presidents and prime ministers at the annual opening session of the UN General Assembly require interpretation and analysis. The foregoing comments provide an elaboration of the speech by the president of the Republic of Cyprus to the international community. The terms used by the president may be familiar to diplomats but not necessarily to the average reader. The president's message was clear. He and his government are committed to the concept of a federal, bizonal, bicommunal republic that would operate in conformity with democratic norms, the UN Security Council resolutions on Cyprus, and European and international law. This is the challenge now facing the EU and the United Nations.

Why the Lack of a Political Settlement?

In the aftermath of the 1974 Turkish invasion and continuing occupation of nearly 37 percent of the Republic of Cyprus, the search for a viable and functional solution to the Cyprus Question continues. It involves the fundamental question of how to structure Cyprus into a viable federal system, in the true constitutional meaning of the term, based on a form of bizonality that would maintain the unity, territorial integrity, and sovereignty of the Republic of Cyprus and protects the rights of all its citizens. Whereas UN peacekeeping in Cyprus has been relatively successful once the 1974 ceasefire line stabilized, UN peacemaking has not been. Consequently, at the time of this writing, Cyprus remains the last occupied and divided country of Europe. Multiple factors account for this situation, including:

- the failure to implement numerous and unanimous Security Council resolutions[4] that contain fundamental provisions for a viable settlement of the Cyprus Question. The failure to implement these resolutions has not only contributed to the current deadlock but also undermined the credibility and moral authority of the United Nations. The UN peacemaking ability remains hostage to the policies and politics of key permanent members and their regional security interests.
- the presence of interests extraneous to the constitutional problems of the Republic of Cyprus. During the Cold War, Britain and the United States failed to act according to the principles of the Charter and of international law because of their strategic needs in the Eastern Mediterranean and the Middle East. Turkey was at the heart of considerations involving NATO's cohesion and effectiveness, the control of the Straits, etc. In the aftermath of the Cold War, energy considerations, Caspian Sea pipelines, the rise of Islamic fundamentalism, and the ongoing crisis in the Middle East had a similar effect on Anglo-American policy on Cyprus. The United States in particular placed its strategic interests above a viable and functional settlement in Cyprus.

Therefore, a case of invasion and continuing occupation has been complicated by external strategic considerations. Consequently, the international factor remains key to a functional and viable settlement.

- the undermining of the United Nations by permanent Security Council members when the organization did not promote their interests in the quest for a Cyprus settlement. Two examples will suffice. The rejection by the United States and Turkey of the 1965 report by UN mediator Galo Plaza[5] and of the 1972 proposal by Secretary-General U Thant for a mediation initiative on Cyprus by nonpermanent members of the Security Council under the chairmanship of France.

- the political aspirations and power-sharing conceptions of the two Cypriot ethnic communities. Cyprus provides a classic case study of the interplay of domestic and external politics in conflict resolution. The minority community came to view the externally imposed independence constitution and, after 1983, the creation of the "TRNC" along with the presence of the Turkish occupation army, as the minimum protection of its rights. The majority Greek Cypriot community saw the 1960 constitution as an externally imposed document that violated cardinal rules of democratic governance and internationally acknowledged human rights. In the post-1974 period, various Anglo-American proposals for a resolution of the Cyprus Question affirmed Turkish and Turkish Cypriot demands. These proposals were promoted through the United Nations. In turn, Greek Cypriots saw these proposals as undermining the sovereignty, unity, and territorial integrity of the republic, while violating the rights of all Cypriot citizens under European law.

- the divergent constitutional constructs advocated by UN mediators, other external parties, Turkey, and the Republic of Cyprus. Up to 1974, the concept of federation had been repeatedly rejected not only by the Greek Cypriots but also by independent external actors. This included Lord Radcliffe in 1956,[6] and UN mediator Galo Plaza in 1965. The federal construct was rejected on the basis of the demographic composition and distribution of Cyprus and the inhumane policy of massive population relocation that would be required in a small island like Cyprus. The forcible population expulsions carried out by the Turkish army following the 1974 invasion made federation on a geographic basis more feasible than in the past. The problem, however, remains that each of the parties and their external supporters has a different understanding of the term "federation." When the United States, which ought to know better from its own constitutional experience, Great Britain, Turkey, the dependent Turkish Cypriot leadership, and UN secretary-general Kofi Annan use the term "federation," in reality imply a confederation of two largely autonomous states. This construct essentially would formalize the outcome of the 1974 Turkish invasion and partition of Cyprus. Consequently, the internationally recognized Republic of Cyprus would be replaced by a loose confederation of two states. The secretary-general's comprehensive plan (Annan-V) presented at the referenda of

24 April 2004, essentially would create a confederation of two largely autonomous states. The absence of a hierarchy of laws, the dependence of the proposed central government on the powers delegated to it by the two component states, and the required consent of the component states in key federal policy areas was clear proof of the nature of the proposed constitutional system. In contrast, the Greek Cypriots have made the painful concession of accepting a federation instead of a unitary form of government as long as it complied with the accepted constitutional terminology and did not violate standards of European law. External mediators and interlocutors studiously avoided use of the term "confederation" in an attempt to avoid the negative images conveyed by the term and to overcome Greek Cypriot fears that confederation simply would legitimize the outcome of the 1974 invasion, occupation, and partition of Cyprus.

- the style of the negotiations. Since the 1974 Turkish invasion, the United States, Great Britain, the United Nations, and Turkey have placed the burden of all concessions on the government of the Republic of Cyprus. Prior to a new round of talks, U.S. and UN representatives would ask the government of Cyprus for a generous concession that would entice Turkey to the negotiating table. This is how in 1977 U.S. presidential emissary Clark Clifford got President Makarios to agree to negotiate on the basis of a bizonal federation. In return, Clifford promised Makarios an active U.S. role in the talks in view of the influence Washington had in Ankara. This concession was expected to elicit flexibility on the part of Turkey. The typical pattern has been that Turkey and the Turkish Cypriots took all these concessions without any reciprocity. This pattern has repeated itself in all rounds of negotiations since 1975. Since then, all Greek Cypriot concessions have been taken for granted by the Turkish Cypriots and Turkey. Meanwhile, no Cypriot government ever demanded that new negotiations commence from a zero base. In 1994, Turkish Cypriot leader Rauf Denktash openly declared that the objective of the negotiations was a confederation and not the "federation" sought by UN mediators. The fear existed that a demand for new negotiations from a zero base could be construed as a sign of intransigence on the part of the authorities of the republic.

- the humane policies of the government of Cyprus. The 1974 Turkish invasion brought about the forcible relocation of nearly 50 percent of the population of the Republic of Cyprus. The government opted not to "palestinianize" the problem of the displaced and the refugees. Instead, it engaged in a dramatic economic development program with minimal external assistance. Within a few years after the invasion, the prosperity of the free areas of the republic was evident. Foreign diplomats praised Cyprus for its success and have used the successful resettlement of the displaced as a means of avoiding the issue of the usurpation of the properties of the displaced in the occupied areas, invalidating the right of return of the displaced to their homes in safety, and avoiding a property recovery system in conformity with the decisions of the European Court of Human Rights.

- the negotiating intransigence of Turkey and of its Turkish Cypriot client leadership who have counted on the external support Turkey has received from the United States, Great Britain, and some of the UN mediators to defuse pressures created by the unresolved Cyprus Question. Turkey's behavior during the negotiations that led to the EU's decision to open accession talks with Turkey on 3 October 2005 is a classic case of how arrogance, intimidation, and threats were utilized in order to attain a negotiating objective. The same have been Turkey's tactics in the negotiations on Cyprus. Turkey and the Turkish Cypriot leaders insist that the Cyprus "problem" was "solved" in 1974. What remains now is the acceptance of that reality and the legal recognition of the "TRNC," the illegal secessionist entity created in the occupied areas under the protection of the Turkish army.

The causes contributing to the lack of a political settlement of the Cyprus Question brings us to the issues in dispute (1974–2005) that will need to be resolved if a viable settlement is to be found.

Issues in Dispute: 1974–2005

As already shown, the Cyprus Question remains one of invasion and continuing occupation. A comprehensive solution for the reunification of the island republic, especially in the aftermath of the accession of Cyprus to the European Union, must reflect democratic norms, the unanimous UN Security Council resolutions on Cyprus, international and European law, and relevant European Court decisions on Cyprus. This section outlines specific issues in dispute. These issues will need to be addressed in any new attempt to reach a viable settlement of the Cyprus Question. These issues include, but are not limited to:

- a new power sharing formula with an effective federal government that can safeguard the unity of the Republic of Cyprus. Such a government should also be able to meet the republic's international and EU obligations. As President Tassos Papadopoulos of Cyprus said to the UN General Assembly on 18 September 2005, a functional working democracy must not require exceptionally taxing efforts for basic governance. Annan-V did not meet that criterion. Moreover, the plan proposed a dysfunctional confederation instead of a federation.
- the implementation of the unanimous UN Security Council resolutions on Cyprus. The failure to implement these resolutions has undermined the credibility of both the UN and the United States, which was the primary sponsor of UN Cyprus settlement initiatives. The United States took great pains to call for the implementation of the resolutions regarding the illegal presence of Syrian troops in Lebanon. However,

it has failed to take a similar stand in the case of the Turkish occupation forces in Cyprus. UN Security Council and General Assembly resolutions call for such a withdrawal.

- the provision of safeguards for the independence and territorial integrity of Cyprus. Any solution must contain effective provisions against the union of Cyprus, in whole or in part, with any other country or in any form of partition or secession. This is an important provision. As discussed in chapter one, the Greek Cypriot unionist movement had ceased to exist by the time of the 1974 Turkish invasion. The Greek Cypriots are solidly committed to the independence, sovereignty, and territorial integrity of the Republic of Cyprus. On the contrary, the opposite is true in the occupied area. The Turkish Cypriot secession of 1983 has been condemned by the international community, and the state that emerged from that secession has been recognized only by Turkey, the sponsor of that state. Moreover, Turkey has repeatedly threatened to incorporate the occupied areas in Turkey as part of its negotiating strategy that aims to create two separate and largely autonomous states in Cyprus. The failed Annan-V plan largely reflected Turkey's objectives. Moreover, Annan-V contained no safeguards for the unity of the new Cypriot state in case the new political system encountered difficulties.

- a Cypriot republic that would enjoy a single sovereignty, international personality, and citizenship in accordance with UN Security Council resolutions and EU rules. Annan-V, the comprehensive plan that was the culmination of the secretary-general's arbitration, could not assure that. The powers granted to the component states subverted these three important principles. Citizenship provisions and the movement of Turks and other foreign nationals through the Turkish Cypriot component state would have complicated Cypriot implementation of EU rules and particularly those under the Schengen Agreement.

- stipulations that would prohibit foreign interference and unilateral right of intervention, and guarantee the withdrawal of foreign forces, other than those stationed in the British bases. UN Security Council resolutions and General Assembly resolutions contain explicit provisions on this subject. Annan-V provided for the eventual reduction of Turkish forces from their current 43,000 troop level. However, under Annan-V Turkey would maintain forces on the island along with the right of unilateral intervention in Cyprus even after Turkey's entry in the EU. This absurd situation made a mockery out of the sovereignty of an EU member state, let alone of the non-intervention provisions of the UN Charter. This is why Secretary-General Annan and his U.S. and British sponsors sought the ratification of these provisions in the referendum of 24 April 2004. If approved by referendum, then no Cypriot government or citizen could ever question the legality of a future Turkish intervention in Cyprus as happened in 1974.

- provisions that would assure the return of the displaced persons in safety to areas currently under Turkish occupation, along with a property recovery system conforming to decisions of the European Court of

Human Rights.[7] This is an important issue. In the Loizidou case, it took considerable effort to assure Turkey's compliance with the European Convention. It should be noted that Turkey has ratified this Convention. Repeated decisions by the European Court of Human Rights have held Turkey responsible for the property usurpation in the occupied areas. These decisions have found the Turkish Cypriot authorities to be only a "subordinate local administration" to that of Turkey. The complicated property restitution system and the limits imposed on the return of the displaced by Annan-V were in conflict with the decisions of the European Court of Human Rights and violated the European Convention and its Protocols.

- the right to acquire property and reside without restrictive quotas based on ethnic or religious criteria in a future federated Cyprus. This would be a natural outcome of the implementation of European law and the proposed European constitution.
- the political equality of the two communities and of all Cypriot citizens as defined under relevant Security Council resolutions and EU laws.
- full respect for the human rights of all citizens of the Republic of Cyprus under the European Convention and its Protocols. Derogations proposed under Annan-V made this issue null and void. Ironically, non-Cypriot EU nationals would have enjoyed full rights under the European Convention, while Cypriot citizens would not have. Examples would include provisions on property rights and the right of movement and settlement, among others. This is why Secretary-General Annan pressed for an approval of these derogations prior to the accession of the Republic of Cyprus to the EU.
- the repatriation of all illegal settlers to Turkey. This important issue cannot be overlooked. Turkey is a signatory of the 1949 Geneva Conventions. In violation of these conventions, Turkey has engaged in a systematic public policy intended to alter the demography of the occupied areas of Cyprus and of the island as a whole. The Anatolian settlers that have been brought into the occupied areas now outnumber the Turkish Cypriots by a 2:1 ratio. Many Turkish Cypriots have opted to emigrate, primarily to England, Germany, and Australia, because of the poor economic and social conditions in the occupied areas. Turkish Cypriots are now a minority in their land. Two major reports by the Council of Europe have fully documented this situation.[8] In contrast, the Turkish authorities have given preferential treatment in housing and employment to the settlers. The settlers from mainland Turkey are dependent on the Turkish government's wishes, and their participation in the political life of the occupied areas has influenced electoral outcomes. The most recent example was their mass participation in the Turkish Cypriot referendum on the secretary-general's plan on 24 April 2004. Their vote was a major factor in the 65 percent approval given to Annan-V in the occupied areas. Repatriation of such illegal settlers is a must, except for a few humanitarian cases involving legitimate cases of intermarriage and children born of such marriages. The secretary-general's comprehensive plan virtually legalized nearly

all Turkish settlers, most of whom would become citizens of the newly created Cypriot state.

- the compatibility of any settlement with the obligations and the rights of the Republic of Cyprus in the European Union. Whatever type of government emerges from any future negotiations must have adequate powers for effective governance, for safeguarding the sovereignty, territorial integrity, and unity of the republic, and for meeting its international and EU obligations. This is a most important issue in the aftermath of the 1 May 2004 accession of Cyprus to the EU. Minority vetoes motivated and controlled by Ankara will destroy the membership of Cyprus in the EU.

- the demilitarization of Cyprus. This idea, which had been floating around since the 1965 Galo Plaza report, was formally proposed by President Spyros Kyprianou of Cyprus and then revived in a more comprehensive form by President George Vassiliou. Finally, the proposal was brought up again in 1993 by President Glafkos Clerides. The intent of the proposal was to break the climate of fear and mistrust created by the military buildup on both sides of the cease-fire line. It should be remembered that the Greek Cypriot buildup had a purely deterrent character in view of the overwhelming advantage the Turkish forces enjoyed in Cyprus. Moreover, these forces could be easily resupplied from bases on Turkey's southern coast, just forty miles north of Cyprus. This proposal was linked to the withdrawal of the Turkish occupation forces along with the disbanding of Turkish Cypriot forces. The proposal involved an expanded UN peacekeeping presence and provided for the savings from defense expenditures to be spent on economic development projects in the island. Unfortunately, Annan-V, while providing for the demilitarization of Cyprus, provided for the continued, albeit reduced, presence of Turkish forces but with intervention rights in the new republic created by the plan. The demilitarization issue will need to be reexamined in the context of the obligations of Cyprus in the emerging common European defense and foreign policy, and the prospective application of Cyprus to join NATO or the Partnership for Peace.

- the issue of the Cypriot missing. Both this and the following issue are primarily humanitarian and involve violations of international and European law. Both must be resolved in any comprehensive solution to the Cyprus Question. The case of the missing involves some 1,479 Greek Cypriots captured by the Turkish forces during the 1974 invasion. Turkey refuses to account for their fate, despite repeated attempts by the United Nations and other humanitarian organizations. The number of the missing is even more staggering when taken in proportion to the 1974 population of Cyprus. Even though the government of the republic has tried to depoliticize this issue and address it outside the framework of the political negotiations, the issue of the missing has not been resolved.

- the matter of the enclaved. Following the massive expulsion of over 160,000 Greek Cypriots from the areas occupied by the Turkish army,

535 Cypriots, primarily from the Karpass Peninsula, chose to remain in their homes in the occupied areas. The living conditions of these enclaved persons remain extremely harsh. Basic foodstuffs are delivered from the free areas of the republic by UN convoys, while they live under constant police surveillance. It is only in the last couple of years that elementary schools have been allowed to operate in the area. Schoolbooks and teachers have to be approved by the occupation authorities. The enclaved cannot work and survive on subsidies from the government of the republic transferred to them through the United Nations. Both issues are a blemish on Turkey's international image, especially at a time when Turkey has opened accession negotiations with the EU.

Issues Raised by Turkey's EU Accession Process

Even though the issues which will be analyzed in this section are not part of the constitutional negotiations for a comprehensive solution to the Cyprus Question, their implications are indicative of Turkey's policies and negotiating stance in the search for such a solution. As of the time of this writing, Turkey does not recognize the internationally recognized Republic of Cyprus or its government. The only state recognized by Turkey is the secessionist entity, the so-called "Turkish Republic of Northern Cyprus," that was created in 1983 under the auspices of the Turkish army.

Turkey signed the Additional Protocol Establishing an Association Between the EU and Turkey. However, it made a unilateral declaration that its signature does not amount to the recognition of the Republic of Cyprus, one of the twenty-five EU members. In its 21 September 2005 response, the EU found Turkey's declaration to be unilateral and with no legal effect on Turkey's obligations under the Protocol,[9] confirmed that the EU recognizes only the Republic of Cyprus, and called on Turkey to live up to its obligations under the Protocol and normalize its relations with all EU members as soon as possible.

Cyprus is one of the EU members participating in the negotiations for Turkey's accession and, along with the other EU members, will take part in the ratification of Turkey's accession treaty, or any other special relationship arrangement that may be the outcome of those negotiations. The Republic of Cyprus has already shown its goodwill, both in December 2004 when Turkey was given a date for the start of accession talks, and in September/October 2005 when the EU agreed to open accession talks with Turkey. Despite the reluctance of a number of EU members over the start and the nature of the accession talks, Cyprus did not exercise its right of veto, alone or in cooperation with others, to stop Turkey's accession process. It should be noted that under the UN secretary-general's comprehensive plan (Annan-V), Cyprus, a sovereign EU member, would be deprived of the right to oppose Turkey's accession to the EU.

Despite EU warnings to Turkey about its obligations under the agreement, Turkey continues to refuse access to its ports, airports, and air corridors to Cypriot vessels and aircraft. This is a direct outcome of Turkey's nonrecognition of the Republic of Cyprus. Turkey has hinted its willingness to consider changes to this policy in return for opening the ports and the airports operated by the illegal regime of the occupied areas. This is another attempt at a de facto recognition of this illegal entity, one more indication of Turkey's policy on the resolution of the Cyprus Question.

On 24 January 2006 Turkish prime minister Recep Tayyip Erdogan and foreign minister Abdullah Gul publicized a set of proposals for the resolution of the Cyprus Question. The proposals had been submitted to UN secretary-general Annan late in December 2005. Foreign Minister Gul and the secretary of Turkey's National Security Council indicated that these proposals were presented after consultation with the leadership of the "TRNC," and that they were being presented on "a take it or leave it basis" to the "Greek Cypriot administration." This is not the place to discuss the details of these proposals, most of which had been unsuccessfully presented in a similar form in May 2005. The reappearance of these proposals met the objective of "staying eleven steps ahead of Cyprus," i.e., it was a purely public relations exercise aimed at influencing international public opinion. In addition, the Turkish proposals sought to get Turkey off the hook from its EU obligations vis-à-vis the Republic of Cyprus, while upgrading the economic and political standing of the illegal regime of the occupied areas. These latest proposals were a classic example of Turkey's bargaining tactics and of the fact that Turkey is not committed to a viable solution to the Cyprus Question. The fulfillment of Turkey's EU obligations is quite different from tactics found in an Anatolian bazaar. The fact that the United States and Britain immediately welcomed Turkey's proposals was not surprising, given the role both countries played in the preparation and presentation of the five Annan plans on Cyprus and the support they extended to Turkey's EU case.

In the same spirit, Turkey continues to exercise its veto to bloc the membership of Cyprus in international organizations, arrangements, and treaties requiring Turkey's consent.[10] Such agreements include, among others, the Missile Technology Control Regime, the Open Skies Treaty, which is vital to the verification of military activities in the Organization of the Black Sea Economic Cooperation (BSEC), and the Organization for Economic Cooperation and Development (OECD), the successor to the OEEC. Turkey has also opposed any connection of Cyprus to NATO or any of its affiliates, and has blocked Cyprus's participation in defense-related activities involving NATO and the EU. These select cases should be of concern to countries such as the United States that have placed emphasis on international cooperation on various security issues. Turkey's actions are indicative of its attitude toward the internationally recognized Republic of Cyprus. Turkey claims that it will recognize a new Cyprus republic that may emerge from a new comprehensive settlement. This confirms Turkey's consistent policy, which seeks the dissolution of the Republic of Cyprus that was created in 1960. Turkey nearly achieved that goal when it succeeded in having last-minute favorable additions made to Annan-V.

Finally, it should be remembered that the issues arising from the implementation of the Customs Union Agreement with the EU are not open to negotiation. They involve Turkey's obligations vis-à-vis all EU members, including Cyprus. Failure on the part of Turkey to meet these obligations will have serious consequences for its quest for EU accession, as the EU Commission has repeatedly stated.

Conclusion

This chapter has outlined the basic dimensions of the Cyprus Question. After more than thirty years, the problem remains one of invasion and occupation. It is also an issue of international legality that affects the credibility of the international legal order, its key institutions, and influential members. The fact that Cyprus is a small and defenseless country gives added significance to this problem in view of the declaratory policies of influential states following the end of the Cold War. The rhetoric of the "new world order" and the "rule of law" has yet to be implemented in practical ways in the case of Cyprus. This chapter has also outlined the issues that need to be addressed in any future settlement of the Cyprus Question and has emphasized the readiness of the Greek Cypriot side to seek a viable and functional solution that conforms to European norms.

CHAPTER THREE

Seeking a Negotiated Settlement, 1999–2004

THE SEARCH for a peaceful, negotiated solution to the Cyprus Question has been the top priority of successive governments of the Republic of Cyprus. This chapter focuses on the 1999–2004 period and the lessons learned from this phase of the negotiation process.

The Greek Cypriot Strategy

The Greek Cypriot negotiating strategy in the 1999–2004 period retained fundamental strategies defined since early in 1964. It also included new elements designed to accommodate the changing international environment of the post-Cold War period. Being a small country and the victim of foreign invasion and occupation since 1974, Cyprus sought legal and political remedies to secure the fundamental goal of protecting its sovereignty, territorial integrity, and unity, as well as to maintain the international recognition of the Republic of Cyprus and its government. These goals did not change after the government of Cyprus accepted in 1977 that a viable and functional solution could be found within the parameters of a bizonal, bicommunal federation.

Despite challenges by Turkey, the government of the Republic of Cyprus has since 1964 successfully defended its international status and the status of the republic. The latest manifestation of this has been the accession of the Republic of Cyprus to the EU on 1 May 2004, and the subsequent statements by the EU following Turkey's unilateral claim that it does not recognize the Republic of Cyprus.

Supported by this recognition, Cyprus relied on the policy of internationalization to keep the issue of the invasion and continuing occupation of Cyprus before the international community. This policy was necessary in order to protect the independence, unity, and territorial integrity of the republic and fend off schemes that run counter to these principles. The United Nations was already engaged in the Cyprus Question since the adoption by the Security Council of resolution 186 (1964) that established the UN peacekeeping force in Cyprus (UNFICYP) and the secretary-general's "mission of good offices."

In addition to the policy of internationalization, Cyprus sought the engagement of the United States at the highest level in its search for a viable solution. Nicosia accurately assessed that Washington had political influence in Ankara, particularly among Turkey's influential military, to affect Turkish policy. This policy involved working with both the U.S. Congress and the executive branch. Congress proved to be more sympathetic to the plight of Cyprus than the executive branch. In the latter case, ill-conceived strategic notions in key agencies about the role and significance of Turkey in U.S. Middle East policy have contributed to the present deadlock.

Another aspect of Cypriot strategy involved the affirmation of the rights of the Republic of Cyprus, its citizens, and institutions by international and national courts. As will be discussed in chapter six, the cases brought by the government of the republic and individual Cypriot citizens to the European Court of Human Rights as well as by the Autocephalous Orthodox Church of Cyprus have become an important part of the Cypriot legal and political case, especially in European institutions. Decisions in these cases have strengthened the ability of the government of Cyprus to reject proposed solutions contradicting fundamental principles of European and international law. Thus, Cypriot strategy displayed a reliance on law, a course typical of small injured states. Looking back at the negotiating cycle that started with the announcement of the G8 formula on Cyprus (Cologne, 20 June 1999) and ended in the Greek Cypriot rejection of Annan-V in the 24 April 2004 referendum, one wonders why two of the pillars of Cypriot strategy ended up not serving Cypriot interests. The two pillars involved the role of the United Nations and that of the United States.

The Changing Role of External Actors

By the middle of the second term of the Clinton administration in Washington, a number of new developments influenced the search for a solution to the Cyprus Question. In a letter to the president of the UN Security Council dated 20 April 1998, Secretary-General Kofi Annan summarized the "new positions" of Turkish Cypriot leader Rauf Denktash. These positions, which had led to the negotiating deadlock and the failure of the secretary-general's mission of good offices, included a mix of old and new ideas. Turkish and Turkish Cypriot officials blatantly argued that the Cyprus "problem" had been "solved" by Turkey's 1974 "intervention" and with the "population exchange" that followed. Thus, they defined their policy on Cyprus in the context of "two states and three problems": (1) the recognition of the existence of two states in Cyprus; (2) at a minimum, the de facto recognition of Denktash's pseudo-state; (3) the acknowledgement of the legitimacy of Denktash's regime and its political procedures; (4) the formation of a confederation of two independent, sovereign, and recognized states; (5) the lifting of the "economic embargo"[1] on the Turkish Cypriots; (6) the continuation of Turkey's military guarantee; and (7) the acceptance of the political equality of the "two sides" in all aspects of the negotiations on Cyprus. In that sense, Denktash's new framework rejected both the intercommunal framework of previous negotiations and the idea of federation. In addition, Denktash demanded that Cyprus's EU application be withdrawn as Cyprus could not become a member while Turkey was not. Denktash described his new positions as the "new political reality."

Ankara was fully aware of Washington's progressive support of most of these ideas. In his mission to Nicosia in May 1998, Richard Holbrooke had promoted the idea of an "acknowledgement' of the Turkish Cypriot political entity, along with the acceptance of the legitimacy of the laws and the institutions established there since 1974. He also suggested that the government of Cyprus acknowledge that it did not speak for the Turkish Cypriots. They were represented by their own leaders, who were elected through their own legitimate procedures. Similar were the views of Sir David Hannay, the British envoy to Cyprus. Hannay and Holbrooke believed that the recommended acknowledgements would provide the necessary momentum for success in a new round of talks. Here we see the story of the concessions demanded of the Greek Cypriots to jump start the stalled negotiations repeating itself.

By 1999, Washington was getting increasingly anxious about the revival of religious fundamentalism and its potential for terrorist activities in the Middle East and elsewhere. This enhanced Turkey's image as America's regional strategic partner. Capitalizing also on the euphoria from the improved climate in Greco-Turkish relations, Washington attempted to sensitize Athens and Nicosia to the need to be more responsive to Turkey's regional needs and domestic problems. Washington also actively promoted Turkey's case for EU accession. Resolving the Cyprus Question would assist Turkey's case in Europe. In the process, Washington quietly attempted to upgrade the standing of the occupation regime in Nicosia in all discussions on Cyprus at the United Nations. The expectation was that such moves would make Turkey and the Turkish Cypriots more amenable to a new round of negotiations. The effect was the opposite. Turkey and the Turkish Cypriots saw these moves as a first step toward recognition.

For the first time, the United States and Britain began coordinating their tactics and ideas for a Cyprus solution. The Anglo-American cooperation and coordination added a new element to the talks. Until then, such cooperation had been sporadic and spasmodic at best.[2] It was evident that these two permanent members of the UN Security Council had finally decided to be involved in a coordinated and sustained manner, if the United Nations was to make progress in the resolution of the Cyprus Question.

Washington also took other steps to control and direct the UN peacemaking efforts on Cyprus. It brought the Cyprus issue to the June 1999 meeting of the G8 in Cologne, Germany.[3] The G8 formula on Cyprus was later endorsed by UN Security Council resolutions 1250 (1999) and 1251 (1999). The formula called the "two sides" to new talks on the basis of four principles: (1) talks without preconditions; (2) discussion of all issues; (3) engagement in sustained talks in good faith until a solution is found; and (4) full consideration of relevant UN resolutions and treaties on Cyprus.

Following the G8 Declaration on Cyprus, Secretary-General Annan also joined the chorus. He added that any future talks ought to address the political status of the Turkish Cypriots. This was in sharp contrast to the stand he had taken on the so-called "new positions" presented by Turkish Cypriot leader Denktash some fourteen months earlier.

The urgency for a new and productive round of talks was underscored in the November 1999 visit of U.S. president Bill Clinton to Athens and Ankara. Pending decisions at the Helsinki summit of the European Union on Turkey's EU candidacy and on the membership of Cyprus increased the urgency of the U.S. initiatives. The aim was to undertake expedited and sustained initiatives that would result in comprehensive, detailed, and binding texts on all aspects of the Cyprus Question, leaving nothing open to future negotiation. In order to meet Turkey's demands, these texts were likely to contain major derogations from European law. This is why the agreement reached would have to be ratified by simultaneous and separate communal referenda in Cyprus prior to the accession of Cyprus to the EU.

The timing of these initiatives was right. The Clinton administration reversed the policy of preceding administrations and supported the accession of Cyprus to the EU. Washington linked accession to the EU with the resolution of the Cyprus Question and with parallel progress on Turkey's application. In view of the progress in its own EU application, Cyprus would have no choice but to participate constructively in a renewed resolution process under UN auspices. The American expectation was that Cyprus would be under pressure to accommodate Turkish and Turkish Cypriot demands on Cyprus in order not to jeopardize its EU candidacy.

Greco-Turkish relations had also improved following the spring 1999 arrest by the Turks, with assistance from the CIA, of Kurdish leader Abdullah Ocalan. Greece had been accused of assisting Ocalan in evading capture. Ocalan's capture brought about personnel changes in the Greek government. George Papandreou, a person favored by Washington, became foreign minister. The mutual assistance the two countries extended to each other in the aftermath of the earthquakes that hit both countries in the summer of 1999 strengthened and improved the new climate in Greco-Turkish relations. However, unless the Cyprus Question was resolved, the risks of conflict in the region remained high. The December 1998 crisis over the proposed placement of Russian S-300 defensive anti-aircraft missiles in Cyprus was clear proof. Moreover, decisions by the European Court of Human Rights in the Loizidou case (1996) had complicated further the imposition of derogations limiting Greek Cypriot property rights in the occupied areas.[4] Turkey's unwillingness to comply with this court ruling was another obstacle on Turkey's road to the EU. A comprehensive settlement would eliminate all outstanding property issues and claims.

It is somewhat ironic, if not also cynical, that while Washington endorsed a solution based on a bizonal, bicommunal federation on Cyprus, in practice the U.S. ideas for a Cyprus solution amounted to a loose confederation of two largely autonomous states on the island. This was close to what Turkey wanted, and was the reality facing the government of Cyprus on the eve of the resumption of the talks at the end of 1999.

The process that led to the presentation of Annan-V in March 2004 started with exploratory talks through the fall of 1999. In November of that year, Kofi Annan presented the two sides with a twenty-point "non-paper" containing fundamental principles to guide the resolution of the problem. This "non-paper" included the commitment that the comprehensive solution would be presented for ratification by separate and simultaneous referenda in both Cypriot communities. The referenda would provide through democratic means the legitimization and approval of the comprehensive solution. The idea of the referenda was not new. It first appeared in 1992 in the secretary-general's "set of ideas." The referenda would be held on the outcome of the negotiated agreement on the Cyprus Question. In 2004, however, the matter that was presented to the referendum vote was the disputed product of the secretary-general's arbitration and not the product of negotiations between the parties. However, this shift in the secretary-general's role from the offer of "good offices" to arbitration was not apparent at the time.

The 12 September 2000 New York meeting of Annan with Cypriot president Glafkos Clerides and Turkish Cypriot leader Rauf Denktash showed in stark terms the reality facing Cyprus. In his opening statement, Annan stated that in the upcoming talks "each side represented itself and no one else and as politically equal." He went on to say that the equality of the two sides would have to be clearly recognized in the comprehensive solution. This rather innocuous statement, whose implications became apparent with the presentation of Annan-V in March 2004, nearly terminated the talks before they even began. Even though it fell short of the recognition demanded by Turkey and the Turkish Cypriots, it was described by them as a historic statement because, for the first time, it equated the standing of the internationally recognized government of the Republic of Cyprus to that of the illegal regime in the occupied areas. Alfred Moses, President Clinton's personal envoy at the talks, characterized the wording of the opening statement as "deliberate ambiguity" intended to bring the Turkish Cypriots to the negotiating table. He also admitted that the secretary-general's opening statement had been made with Washington's knowledge and consent.[5]

The secretary-general's personal representative in Cyprus, Alvaro de Soto, was assisted by Tom Weston of the U.S. Department of State, Alfred Moses, President Clinton's envoy, and Lord David Hannay of the United Kingdom. Annan's legal and political team that prepared the various "non-papers" that were presented to the parties and ultimately drafted the five versions of the Annan plan had steady guidance and technical support from the United States and Britain. Washington and London also tested their ideas on the parties and lobbied hard to gain their acceptance. This included active lobbying of the governments of Athens and Ankara, in the belief that they in turn would influence their respective communities on Cyprus.

Even though this round of talks ended in deadlock in January 2001 and did not resume in earnest until the following year, the direction of the talks was clear. The wording of the "non-papers" presented to the parties did not conform to the Security Council resolutions or to the decisions of the European Court of Human Rights on Cyprus. New words cropped in, including: (1) the "common state": the entity that would replace the internationally recognized Republic of Cyprus; (2) the equal status of the "component states": the new Cypriot republic would be created from two states, at Turkey's insistence; (3) the abandonment of the principle of a "just solution" for an "equitable" solution, opening the way to compromises away from the principles of the UN resolutions, European law, etc.; (4) the replacement of references about the government and the Republic of Cyprus by words like "the two sides"; and (5) the appearance of concepts such as that of "internal sovereignty" for each of the component states. This was of importance to Turkey and the Turkish Cypriots, as it provided components of statehood to the illegal entity in the occupied areas.

These "non papers" signified another change in tactics in the upcoming negotiations. The secretary-general offered to submit his own proposals and texts to the "two sides," rather than have them exchange and negotiate over their own position papers. The responses of the two sides to these papers would assist the United Nations in the formulation of a comprehensive plan for the resolution of the problem. This was the beginning of the change in the role of the secretary-general from the provision of "good offices" to arbitration. His role as arbitrator became apparent in February 2004. Coupled with the commitment of the two parties to submit the comprehensive solution to separate and simultaneous referenda, the stage was set for the events of 2004. This, however, was not apparent at the time.

Ever since the 1974 Turkish invasion of Cyprus, the understanding was that there would be territorial v. constitutional tradeoffs by the "two sides" in any comprehensive solution. The clear implication was that the greater the amount of territory restored to Greek Cypriot control, the looser the federal structure would become. The criteria for territorial concessions, until then, included: issues of security affecting the Turkish Cypriot "state"; the population ratio between the two "states"; the economic viability of the Turkish Cypriot "state"; and developmental issues affecting the Turkish Cypriot "state." For example, the Tymbou Airport in the occupied areas would remain under Turkish Cypriot control as it was important for the economic development of the Turkish Cypriot "state."

By November 2000, however, a new, additional criterion entered the UN vocabulary. This was the need to balance the maximum number of Greek Cypriots returning to areas formerly under Turkish Cypriot control with the Turkish Cypriot population and to consider the "least inconvenience" of the Turkish Cypriot population (including the illegal settlers) residing in these areas. In practical terms, this latest criterion seriously limited the territorial adjustment in any future settlement.

The "non-papers" presented by the United Nations contained serious derogations from accepted European standards in the rights of movement, settlement, and property ownership. They also left in place most of the illegal Turkish settlers, while creating a loose confederation of two largely autonomous states. The godparents of these ideas were Richard Holbrooke and U.S. ambassador Tom Weston, along with Lord Hannay of Britain.

A final consideration in understanding the international environment of the period from 1999 to 2004 has to do with the issue of terrorism, the attacks of 11 September 2001 in the United States and the wars in Iraq and Afghanistan. Even though the United States received wide European support following the 11 September attacks, the U.S. decisions leading to the 2003 invasion of Iraq created serious divisions in the Western alliance and undermined the credibility and authority of the United Nations. Between 2002 and 2004 the Cyprus Question entered its most critical phase with the Anglo-

American commitment to "close the book" on Cyprus. The search for a Cyprus solution attained a new urgency. The question had been on the UN agenda for decades. A successful resolution through the United Nations would prove Washington's support for the organization and ability to work with it and other European countries to resolve a long-standing international problem. This, then, was an additional reason why both Washington and London expended so much time and effort to bring about the five plans on Cyprus presented by Secretary-General Kofi Annan and his negotiating team.

The Changing Role of the UN Secretary-General: From "Good Offices" to Arbitration

The mission of "good offices" of the secretary-general in the case of Cyprus was defined by Security Council resolutions 186 (1964) and 367 (1975), among others. These resolutions were adopted under Chapter 4 of the UN Charter.[6] The "mission of good offices" has traditionally been conceived as a means of facilitating discussions and negotiations between disputing parties. At best, under this function, the secretary-general and/or his representative could produce constructive ideas for use by disputing parties in their negotiations. At no time, however, did the parties request or agree to the expansion of Kofi Annan's role, nor did the UN Security Council directly authorize such an expansion. The change in the secretary-general's role came about in 2004. It was a unilateral act imposed on the parties as a condition for the resumption of the talks in February of 2004. The previous section has already shown trends indicative of this shift in the secretary-general's role. This change from "good offices" to arbitration appears to have been motivated by the deadlock and the inability of the parties to resolve their differences and by the urgency felt in the United States and Britain to resolve this issue prior to the accession of Cyprus to the EU.

The talks that culminated in the March 2004 Burgenstock, Switzerland, negotiations on Cyprus and the 24 April 2004 failed referendum on Annan-V started on 16 January 2002. On that date, President Glafkos Clerides, on behalf of the Greek Cypriot community, and Turkish Cypriot leader Rauf Denktash met face-to-face in Nicosia to jump-start the talks. However, these talks failed to make substantive progress, given the Turkish and Turkish Cypriot demands that have already been identified. In an attempt to secure an agreement by the 12–13 December 2002 Copenhagen EU Summit which would decide on the accession of Cyprus to the EU, Kofi Annan presented on 11 November 2002 a comprehensive plan on Cyprus. This came to be known as Annan-I. Following reaction by the parties, the plan was revised and resubmitted on 10 December 2002. This is the plan known as Annan-II. Both of these plans were rejected by Turkey and the Turkish Cypriots. Consequently, the secretary-general continued revisions to his plan in an attempt to secure Turkey's acceptance. The third version of his plan, Annan-III, was presented to the parties on 26 February 2003.

Annan asked to meet the "leaders of the two communities" at the Hague on 10 and 11 March 2003 to inform him if they were prepared to submit Annan-III to separate and simultaneous referenda in their communities. The use of the term "leaders of the two communities" was deliberate. It avoided the status distinction of the internationally recognized president of the Republic of Cyprus and that of the leader of the unrecognized entity in the occupied areas. Each "leader" spoke on behalf of his "community." The Republic of Cyprus was represented by its newly elected president, Tassos Papadopoulos, who had not yet been sworn into office, and by the outgoing president, Glafkos Clerides. Papadopoulos agreed to submit Annan-III to a referendum, provided the Cypriot public had a complete negotiated framework in place for their consideration; Greece and Turkey had reached an agreement on revisions to the 1960 independence agreements and the related Treaty of Guarantee; and there was adequate time for public discussion. Annan-III was rejected by the Turkish Cypriots and Turkey as it fell short of Turkey's goals.

A number of important developments took place in and around Cyprus during this time. The United States and Turkey engaged in a rancorous debate over Turkey's denial of access rights by U.S. forces for the invasion of Iraq and the use of U.S. bases on Turkish soil in that war. Despite U.S. support for Turkey's goals on Cyprus and significant financial incentives, Turkey refused to cooperate with the United States.

Massive Turkish Cypriot demonstrations took place in the occupied areas against the regime of Turkish Cypriot leader Rauf Denktash and his Ankara endorsed policies. The two largest demonstrations (14 January and 26 February 2003) were legitimized by the presence of representatives of foreign embassies accredited to the Republic of Cyprus, especially those of the United States and Britain. Their presence was a clear indication that both considered Denktash to be the obstacle in the search for a solution to the Cyprus Question. This was the beginning of a regime change operation that some fifteen months later culminated in new leadership in the Turkish Cypriot community. The demonstrations favored the acceptance of Annan-III and the accession of Cyprus to the EU. Meanwhile, as expected, the Republic of Cyprus, along with nine other candidate countries, signed the EU Treaty of Accession in a ceremony in Athens, Greece, on 16 April 2003. Under the terms of the Accession Treaty, the implementation of the *acquis communautaire* in the occupied areas was suspended until the reunification of the island was achieved. It should be noted that the EU recognizes only the Republic of Cyprus as created by the 1960 independence agreements.

Growing Turkish Cypriot public opposition to Denktash and his rejection of Annan-III, along with the signature of the EU Treaty of Accession by the government of Cyprus, forced the Turkish Cypriot leader and his Turkish sponsors to partially lift restrictions on the movement of persons and goods across the cease-fire line. These restrictions had been imposed by the occupation forces since the 1974 Turkish invasion. Since the easing of the restrictions, thousands from both sides of the cease-fire line have crossed peacefully. By this decision, the Turkish Cypriot side also expected an economic shot in the arm by the money that would be spent by Greek Cypriots visiting their ancestral homes and by the prospect of EU funding. Thousands of Turkish Cypriots cross daily to work in the free areas of the republic, to claim passports and other documents issued by the Republic of Cyprus, to receive free medical care, and to visit religious shrines. These peaceful crossings have destroyed the myth cultivated for years by Turkish propaganda that the two communities cannot live together. It is also ironic that, despite the renunciation of the Republic of Cyprus by the regime of the occupied areas, thousands of Turkish Cypriots have sought documents issued by the Republic of Cyprus such as passports and identity cards. Until 2003 Turkish Cypriots were prohibited by the occupation authorities to possess or use such documents, even though they were entitled to do so as citizens of the Republic of Cyprus.

These measures and developments were no substitute for a comprehensive solution. The U.S. government, once more, seized the negotiating initiative. It capitalized on the readiness of the government of the Republic of Cyprus to participate on a new round of talks on the basis of Annan-III. It also felt the need to mend fences with Turkey in the aftermath of the March 2003 confrontation over Iraq. Turkey's government was under the leadership of the Islamic Justice and Development Party (AKP), led by Recep Tayyip Erdogan. His presence in Ankara served American regional objectives quite well. Prime Minister Erdogan was presented as a model of a democratic Islamic leader in the troubled region of the Middle East. He was invited to visit the White House in January 2004. During this visit Erdogan expressed his readiness to engage in a new round of talks on Cyprus with Annan-III as a "point of reference," rather than as a basis for negotiations. The latter was what the government of Cyprus had proposed and the secretary-general insisted on. It appears that Turkey's change of heart over the value of Annan-III was the result of assurances of American support for Turkey's positions in any upcoming talks. Next, in similar meetings, the Bush administration convinced Secretary-General Annan to call for a resumption of talks on Cyprus in New York. This was also a change in the position of Annan who, until then, had found that a major gap separated the positions of the two sides. The secretary-general had been unwilling to undertake a new initiative until he had solid reason to believe that the parties exhibited the political will necessary for a successful outcome.

In his letter of invitation dated 4 February 2004, the secretary-general insisted that his plan of 26 February 2003 (Annan-III) was a carefully balanced package.[7] He called for the commitment of the leadership of the two Cypriot communities to finalize his plan without reopening basic principles or core trade-offs. This would also require the backing of Greece and Turkey, two of the 1960 guarantor powers. The secretary-general had as his objective the resolution of the question prior to the 1 May 2004 accession of Cyprus to the EU. He presented an unrealistically narrow and rigid negotiating timeline to achieve each step of his proposed negotiating process, including appointments to transitional organs of the proposed new republic. The most critical paragraph of this invitation letter indicative of the changing role of the secretary-general was item 4 on page 4. This paragraph stated that

> It is clearly desirable that the text should emerge completed from the negotiations between the parties by the dates specified above. However, should that not happen, I would, by March 31, make any indispensable suggestions to complete the text. Naturally, I would only do this with the greatest of

reluctance, and indeed I very much hope that this prospect would spur the parties to approach the effort with the determination required to come to terms in a timely fashion.

The invitation letter even included the text of how the question to be presented to the voters would be phrased. It called for separate and simultaneous referenda to be held on 21 April 2004. This was a major political blunder, given the significance of the date in Greece and Cyprus. It was on that date in 1967 that a group of Greek army colonels, using a NATO emergency plan, seized control of the Greek government. It was the colonels' short-lived coup in Cyprus on 15 July 1974 that triggered the Turkish invasion. Following protests, the date was changed to 24 April to account for Greek and Greek Cypriot sensitivities.

In meetings held in New York between 10 and 13 February 2004, the president of the Republic of Cyprus acting as leader of the Greek Cypriot community and the Turkish Cypriot leader, with support from Greece, Turkey, Britain, and the United States, agreed to the secretary-general's formula. Neither side had any choice on the matter, given that the binding arbitration was the only acceptable way for the engagement of the secretary-general in a new round of talks.

On 13 February, outlining the agreed formula for the talks, Annan's spokesman reiterated that "as a final resort, in the event of continuing and persistent deadlock, the parties have invited the secretary-general to use his discretion to finalize the text to be submitted to referenda on the basis of his plan." The secretary-general also welcomed the readiness of the EU to accommodate the terms of a settlement. Both of these decisions proved to be critical for what happened on 24 April.

As shown in this chapter, from early on the Greek Cypriots had placed trust and confidence in the United Nations and the conduct of the Secretariat under the UN Charter and international law. As Claire Palley has amply documented, the shift from facilitator to a party in the dispute undermined the credibility of the UN.[8] Instead of remaining "above the fray," the Secretariat became identified with the positions of some of the parties in the dispute. Its subsequent criticism of the Greek Cypriot rejection of Annan-V in a democratic referendum and the implied threats extended by the secretary-general's representative, Alvaro de Soto, to avert such a rejection, destroyed the objectivity of the process. It showed the commitment of the United Nations to particular positions favored by Turkey, the United States, and Britain. The Greek Cypriots realized, a bit too late, how the secretary-general became a party to the dispute and betrayed the principles and the resolutions of the United Nations, the organization he represents.

The change in the secretary-general's role, coupled with extremely tight negotiating deadlines and Turkey's intransigence, contributed to the absence of serious negotiations either in Nicosia or in Burgenstock, Switzerland, in the spring of 2004. In order to gain Turkey's consent, nearly all of its demands were incorporated arbitrarily in both Annan-IV and Annan-V. Turkey and the United States agreed to grant the EU only an observer status in the talks, while getting the commitment of the EU to accommodate the derogations from European law that were included in Annan's plans. This explains the urgency felt in Washington, London, and New York to complete the resolution process prior to the accession of Cyprus to the EU. In this manner, the serious derogations from EU law and court decisions incorporated in Annan's plan could be justified as a private agreement between the parties arrived at prior to the accession of Cyprus to the EU. The secretary-general's comprehensive plan, Annan-V, consisted of nearly ten thousand pages. It should be noted that this complex document was not available in its totality on the UN website until hours before the referendum.[9] Cypriots were expected to vote on this complex, comprehensive plan on 24 April, days before the 1 May accession of the Republic of Cyprus to the EU.

The mere size and complexity of this document is an indication that it was the product of prior preparation. Alvaro de Soto's legal team, assisted by U.S. and British experts and diplomats, had been working on these documents for years, behind the back of the Cypriots. Their collective work became the plan known as Annan-V. The Turkish Cypriot rejection of all previous UN proposals may have put Greek Cypriot minds at ease, despite the leaks about the changing views of the UN and the United States, especially after the deadlocked talks that started in 1999. The events of 2004 proved how wrong the Greek Cypriot assumptions and strategies had been regarding the role of the United States and the United Nations, let alone Turkey's negotiating behavior.

Annan-V: The Process

Simplified summaries of the comprehensive plan were circulated in English, Greek, and Turkish by the United Nations, various NGOs, and other media both in and outside Cyprus. The United Nations and the United States were actively involved in the promotion of the plan in Cyprus. U.S. involvement in this promotion was quite controversial in view of the millions of dollars spent on this process. The U.S. embassy in Nicosia gave approval only to projects proposed by Cypriots and others who were in favor of Annan-V. No projects were funded that were critical of the comprehensive plan. U.S. funds were channeled under the deceptive umbrella in Nicosia of UNOPS (UN Office for Project Services) and could only be dispersed with the approval of the U.S. embassy. A detailed evaluation report for the U.S. Agency for International Development, the sponsor of the program, has given revealing details of this promotional scheme.[10]

In the more critical phase of the negotiations and the time leading to the 24 April referendum, U.S. and British officials also attempted to influence the Cypriot political leadership in order to gain their endorsement of Annan's arbitration. Telephone calls from the U.S. secretary of state and others to the speaker of the House of Representatives and other politicians were intended to overcome the opposition of the elected president of the Republic of Cyprus and his government. This type of interference in the domestic affairs of a democratic but small European state was clearly unethical and unacceptable. It was judged so by the vast majority of the Greek Cypriots as well.

The narrow timelines established by the secretary-general, coupled with the unholy alliance of the Secretariat, the United States, Britain, and Turkey, doomed the negotiations. In reality, there were no negotiations in the accepted meaning of the term. The first phase, known as the Nicosia phase, lasted between 19 February and 22 March 2004. This phase primarily involved the work of the technical committees, which examined fiscal issues that were largely overlooked in the preparation of Annan-III, reviewed federal laws and treaties, and discussed the federal executive and the representation of Cyprus in the EU so that the new Cypriot state could speak with one voice. There were also discussions regarding the creation of a court of first instance at the federal level to address constitutional and federal administrative issues. It was during these talks that Turkey challenged the economic zone agreement signed between Cyprus and Egypt on 17 February 2003, successfully demanded that the ratification by Cyprus of the 1936 Montreux Treaty on the regime of the Straits be annulled, and demanded controls on the continental shelf of Cyprus, coastal security, and so on. During this phase of the talks, Britain also attempted to expand its rights in the sovereign base areas and adjacent waters. Alvaro de Soto, Annan's representative, controlled the agenda of the talks under the guise of keeping the discussions within the parameters of Annan-III.

The second and third phases of the talks took place in the isolated village of Burgenstock, Switzerland. During the second phase, Greece and Turkey were to assist the parties to finalize the proposed document. They were to remain there in the third phase only as advisers and observers. In reality, this did not happen. The late arrival of Turkish prime minister Erdogan made him a major participant until the end. While Annan, Alvaro de Soto and his team, along with American and British diplomats carefully orchestrated the meetings, they also took great pains to keep other influential actors outside the conference. A high-level Russian delegation was deliberately kept away and was only allowed limited contact with representatives of the government of Cyprus. The Burgenstock reality was that there were no negotiations in the traditional sense of the term.

At Burgenstock, the regime change that had gotten underway in occupied Nicosia in the spring of the preceding year came to completion. Turkish Cypriot "prime minister" Mehmet Ali Talat replaced Rauf Denktash as Turkish Cypriot leader. Denktash's son, Serdar, became "foreign minister" of the "TRNC." On 27 May 2004, a month after the referendum, Talat received the official blessing of the United States, which named him "leader" of the Turkish Cypriot community.

On 29 March 2004, Kofi Annan presented his "overall bridging proposal," the plan known as Annan-IV. With hardly any negotiation and having incorporated nearly all of the eleven points presented by Turkish ambassador Ugur Ziyal three days earlier, on 31 March the secretary-general presented the parties with his final plan, Annan-V. This was the plan that was to be presented at the 24 April referenda. The plan consisted of nearly ten thousand pages of complicated legal text.[11] The manner by which the comprehensive plan was prepared, dictated, and presented almost assured its rejection by the Greek Cypriots. In an emotional speech to the Greek Cypriot electorate on 8 April, the president of the Republic of Cyprus explained the reasons why he could not support the plan. President Papadopoulos's speech was criticized by the United Nations, the United States, and other Cypriot and non-Cypriot supporters of Annan-V. However, public opinion polls prior to the president's speech showed nearly 70 percent of Greek Cypriots disapproving the plan. The plan was so one-sided in favor of Turkey that it simply legitimized the outcome of the 1974 Turkish invasion. In view of the nature of the plan and its consequences for the internationally recognized Republic of Cyprus, one wonders why the United Nations, the United States, and the United Kingdom acted in this manner. It was as if they wanted the Greek Cypriots to say "no" so as to allow them to justify actions in Cyprus favoring Turkey.

Two concluding comments will close this section. The first is that contrary to allegations by the United Nations and the United States, the Greek Cypriot media carried out an informed and free debate on this plan. Cyprus is a country with an open, competitive, democratic political system. Open political discussions and debate on all issues is the hallmark of Cypriot press, TV, and radio. This was also the case with discussion of the Annan plan in the short time available prior to the separate and simultaneous referenda.

The second concluding point has to do with the secretary-general and his plan. When the February 2004 cycle of the negotiations began, Annan indicated that if either or both communities rejected it, his plan would be off the table. This not only has not happened, but we continue to hear that any future negotiations will have to take place on the basis of the rejected Annan-V. This point will be examined later in this volume.

Two other aspects of this process increased Greek Cypriot suspicions. The first involved the threat of "dire consequences" that would follow a Greek Cypriot rejection of the plan. These threats were frequently repeated by UN envoy Alvaro de Soto. Similar threats were made by the American envoy, Ambassador Tom Weston, starting with his arrival statement at the Larnaca airport just before the commencement of the February 2004 talks. Ironically, the referendum on the UN plan had been advertised as the democratic affirmation of the resolution of the Cyprus Question. The threats emanating from the United Nations and the United States made a mockery of the democratic choice theory. Greek Cypriot suspicions were also raised by last-minute promises of financial assistance to mitigate the cost of reunification under Annan-V. A hastily convened donors conference just prior to the referendum fell seriously short of expectations. Pledges amounted close to $750 million, even though the cost of reunification was estimated to be closer to $15 billion. Greek Cypriots knew that given the state of and the demands on the international economy and the relative affluence of the free areas of the republic, the economic cost of reunification would be borne by Greek Cypriot taxpayers. Turkey, which invaded, occupied, and introduced the settlers in Cyprus, was absolved and would not bear any of the cost of its actions.

The 24 April 2004 Referenda

The outcome of the simultaneous but separate referenda of 24 April 2004 was predictable. By a vote of 75.8 percent, the Greek Cypriot electorate rejected Annan-V. In contrast, 64.9 percent of the Turkish Cypriot voters approved the plan. It should be noted that the Turkish settlers, who are not Cypriot citizens, not only participated in the referendum in the occupied areas but made up a significant percentage of the total votes cast in favor of the plan. The Greek Cypriot vote came from voters across the board in terms of party affiliation, gender, and age. The Greek Cypriot "no" vote was not a vote against reunification or reconciliation. It was a rejection of a process that led to a one-sided plan perceived harmful to their legitimate rights and to the survival of their internationally recognized state. It was a rejection of a plan that failed to provide genuine reunification of the country, its economy, and society.

The vote in favor of Annan-V by the Turkish Cypriots and the settlers is easier to explain:

- It reflected the rejection of the authoritarian policies of Rauf Denktash, supported by the Turkish Army, which for decades ran a regimented system that intimidated dissenters. The unraveling of his regime started in the externally supported demonstrations of January/February 2003.
- They anticipated the economic benefits of EU membership and Greek Cypriot economic support. This was important in view of the poor economic conditions in the occupied areas.
- Annan-V maintained the illegal Turkish Cypriot "state." It also granted extended veto powers to the Turkish Cypriot community. Under the plan, Turkish Cypriots would control affairs not only in their own component state but also of the so-called "United Republic of Cyprus."
- Nearly all Turkish settlers would remain in the Turkish Cypriot component state, either by the extension of citizenship or of permanent residence. Those desiring to leave would receive appropriate compensation. The vague provisions of the Alien and Immigration Law would likely allow the continued influx of settlers from Turkey.
- The plan provided for continued Turkish military presence in Cyprus with intervention rights, even after Turkey's EU accession. Even though under Annan-V the Turkish military presence in Cyprus would be gradually reduced, the presence of major Turkish military facilities within forty miles of Cyprus provided an additional assurance to the Turkish Cypriots and the Turkish settlers.
- Turkey retained its guarantor status and intervention rights in all of the territory of the new and demilitarized "United Republic of Cyprus." This had been a standing demand of Turkey and of the Turkish Cypriot leadership.
- The economic burden of reunification would be born by the Greek Cypriots and the international community.

Several legitimate reasons explain the Greek Cypriot "no" vote in the referendum:

- The negotiation process included rigid deadlines, no real time for discussion of a most complex legal document, and threats expressed or implied by Alvaro de Soto and U.S. ambassador Tom Weston, if the Greek Cypriots did not accept the proposed plan. Many of these points have been developed earlier in this volume. The threats expressed by foreign interlocutors showed their lack of understanding of the Greek Cypriot political consciousness and their independent mentality. Instead of intimidating, these threats provoked the Greek Cypriot sense of independence and resistance.

- The derogations from the European Convention deprived all Cypriots of fundamental rights. At the same time, other EU nationals residing in Cyprus would enjoy all their rights under the European Convention. Annan-V would terminate all property cases pending before the European Court of Human Rights. Moreover, Cypriot nationals could not bring future cases to the European Court of Human Rights on issues arising from the implementation of the Annan plan. This was an indication of the finality of Annan-V.

- The plan violated the European Convention by denying the right of Cypriots to acquire and enjoy their property and live wherever they chose, as other EU nationals could, without restrictive quotas based on ethnicity and religion. Discrimination based on ethnicity and religion violated the European Convention and its associated Protocols, as well as key provisions of the emerging European Constitution.

- The internationally recognized Republic of Cyprus would be dissolved and replaced by a loose confederation of two largely autonomous states. The two "states" would be joined in a new "United Republic of Cyprus" with a new flag and a new national anthem. There was no guarantee that, in case of difficulty in the implementation of Annan-V, Cyprus would not break up into two separate states.

- The functionality of the "United Republic of Cyprus" was questionable. The plan contained dysfunctional provisions on the executive, legislature, and judiciary. The provisions were complicated further by various minority vetoes. Moreover, non-Cypriot third parties, unaccountable to the Cypriot public, would cast deciding votes in key policy areas. All these provisions violated basic democratic procedures.

- Despite the description of the new republic as a federation, the plan clearly created a confederation of two largely autonomous states. This was manifested by a deliberate absence of a hierarchy of laws in the proposed "federal" system. In addition, federal powers emanated from the component states and were based on the consent of these states. This opened the way to jurisdictional conflicts. It also enhanced the divisive nature of the proposed new policy.

- There were inadequate guarantees ensuring that the commitments undertaken by the parties, particularly Turkey, would be carried out.

- The economic cost of the proposed settlement was estimated to be close to $15 billion. It involved the cost of economic convergence, reconstruction, property compensation, compensation to settlers, and monetary policy. Turkey, whose military invasion divided the island and created economic chaos in the occupied areas, was absolved of any financial responsibility for its actions in Cyprus. The hastily called donors conference on the eve of the referendum was seen as nothing more than a last minute bribe to encourage a favorable vote by the Greek Cypriots on Annan-V. The conference pledged some $750 million, a mere drop in the bucket in the cost of reunification. The Greek Cypriots, the victims of Turkey's aggression, knew well that they would be the ones bearing the cost of reunification.
- Security issues were extremely important. They involved the gradual reduction and continued presence of Turkish troops with expanded intervention rights in Cyprus, even after Turkey joined the EU. This was an unprecedented situation in twenty-first-century Europe. In violation of the UN Charter, a non-EU member had the right to station troops on the soil of an EU member and to intervene at will in the affairs of an independent and sovereign state. This was even more dangerous, considering that Cyprus would be totally demilitarized and that the "United Republic of Cyprus" would be excluded from the common European Defense Policy.
- The definition of citizenship was such that it assured that nearly all illegal Turkish settlers would remain in Cyprus as citizens and/or permanent residents. Moreover, the Alien and Immigration Law opened the way to future Turkish settlers entering Cyprus.
- The property provisions of the Annan plan violated essential rights under the European Convention and its Protocols, confirmed the property usurpation in the occupied areas, and overturned important precedent-setting European Court of Human Rights decisions.[12]
- The plan expanded Britain's rights in the sovereign base areas and the republic's territorial waters. These provisions had nothing to do with the constitutional settlement in Cyprus. It was an opportunity for Britain to expand the rights it obtained unilaterally in 1959 as a precondition for Cyprus's independence. Economic considerations involving possible underwater resources may have been behind these moves.
- On the insistence of Turkey, the plan deleted the ratification by the Republic of Cyprus of the 1936 Montreux Convention on navigation through the Straits. This was significant, as Cyprus is a major commercial maritime power. Turkey in recent years has tried to amend the terms of the 1936 Convention protecting the freedom of navigation through the Straits using environmental and other justifications. Excluding a major maritime power from that treaty was one more step in Turkey's quest to gain full control of an international waterway. Moreover, the plan granted Turkey near veto powers on the continental shelf of Cyprus and questioned economic zone agreements between Cyprus and neighboring states. This was one more attempt by Turkey to assert its hegemonial role in Cyprus and limit Cypriot sovereignty.

These points show clearly some of the key reasons for the rejection of Annan-V by the Greek Cypriots. It was a proposal serving Turkish interests and not the common interests of all Cypriots. President Papadopoulos summarized the situation best when after the referendum he said that "the only real beneficiary of this plan would have been Turkey." While all of Turkey's demands were adopted in the final plan on the last day of the Burgenstock talks, basic concerns of the Greek Cypriots were totally disregarded. The foreign interlocutors were anxious to bring Turkey on board and ensure a "yes" vote by the Turkish Cypriot community. In the process, they ignored the fact that the majority Greek Cypriot community also had to be convinced to vote "yes" on the plan. The failure to consider, let alone address, legitimate Greek Cypriot concerns led to the rejection of Annan-V by the Greek Cypriots.

One more question needs to be answered in this section. Why were the international interlocutors so insistent on having their plan ratified by separate and simultaneous communal referenda? There were at least three reasons behind this insistence:

- It removed the stigma that the final settlement was imposed on the Greek Cypriots through the secretary-general's binding arbitration. Kofi Annan wanted to avoid the precedent of the 1959 Zurich and London Agreements. Greek Cypriots had complained that the independence agreements were imposed on them under the threat of the partition of Cyprus.
- It legitimized and affirmed Turkey's intervention rights. Under Annan-V, Turkey would retain these rights even after its entry in the EU. Greek Cypriots had questioned the legality of Turkey's intervention rights and the use of force against Cyprus in 1974 which Turkey justified under the terms of the 1959 agreements. Approval by referendum would remove any future legal questions.
- All derogations from EU law and treaties would also be legitimized. This would make difficult any future demand for changes in these derogations.

The Lessons Learned from the 1999–2004 Experience

The process that started in 1999 with the G8 Cologne declaration on Cyprus ended in Nicosia with the results of the 24 April 2004 referendum. The secretary-general and his interlocutors presented the referendum as the democratic affirmation of the outcome of their arbitration/mediation. If, indeed, they believe in the democratic process, they should also be willing to accept and respect its outcome, which was arrived at in a free and open debate. The early postreferendum expressions of disappointment, disapproval, and threats to the Republic of Cyprus by UN, U.S., and British officials contradict the democratic argument. UN and U.S. officials repeatedly called on Greek Cypriot voters to "rethink their vote" and accept the plan as it stands, especially because of its unconditional acceptance by the Turkish Cypriots. In the last year, the same diplomats have come to accept the reality that "some changes" may be needed to account for Greek Cypriot concerns without affecting the overall balance of the plan. They indicate readiness to examine possible cosmetic changes to the plan and clarifications on security and economic issues, without touching on substantive positions of the comprehensive plan. Such absolute positions may amount to negotiating tactics by the UN and the United States. However, these positions show how far they are from the reasons for the Greek Cypriot rejection of Annan-V, and for the fact that Cyprus is now a full-fledged member of the EU with rights and responsibilities that cannot be diluted in order to satisfy the interests of outside parties.

The last phase of the negotiation process from February to April 2004 will become a classic study of how not to negotiate. Leaving aside the content of Annan-V, the combination of threats, unrealistic deadlines amounting to an ultimatum, externally funded propaganda activities in a sovereign European country, last-minute financial promises, attempts to bypass the legitimately elected government of an internationally recognized state, and external interventions in the affairs of both communities backfired at the end of the day. Only in the case of a small and weak country would such tactics ever have been attempted. In the case of Cyprus they failed, and rightly so. External interlocutors must reflect on their actions that led to the outcome of the 24 April 2004 referenda, instead of blaming those who freely exercised their democratic rights and chose to say "no." External interlocutors must consider what they may have done wrong. Were there miscalculations on their part and on the part of their staff? What could they have done differently? Why did they fail to take into account the concerns and needs of the Greek Cypriot community?

U.S. and UN officials, both before and after the referendum, characterized Annan-V as the "last opportunity" to solve the Cyprus Question. They also claimed that the international community would lose interest, and that there would never be another comprehensive plan on Cyprus. Good, credible diplomats never say never. What is needed is a careful reassessment of how we got to this point in the Cyprus Question and what happens now that Cyprus is an EU member. It is clear that the solution must conform to the Security Council resolutions on Cyprus, to European law and court decisions, and to international law. In this manner, a solution can be found serving the interests of all Cypriots rather than those of outside parties.

CHAPTER FOUR

Why the Status Quo Is Not an Option: Prospects for a Viable Solution

AS SHOWN EARLIER, for legitimate reasons and in a democratic manner the Greek Cypriots turned down Annan-V. Even though the UN initiatives in the period 1999–2004 did not resolve the Cyprus Question, the Greek Cypriots do not believe that the referendum was the end of the road. As the president of the Republic of Cyprus has said, the result of the referendum must act as a catalyst for reunification and not as a pretext for further division. This chapter will analyze this important statement, because the government of the Republic of Cyprus does not consider the status quo as an option. It is committed to reaching a viable and functional solution that will provide a prosperous and secure future for all the citizens of the republic, ensure respect for the human rights and fundamental freedoms of all Cypriots, and allow the government to function effectively within the EU.

Many in the international community were unfamiliar with the detailed provisions of Annan-V and the plan's implications and consequences for the future of the republic and its citizens. This is why many expressed disappointment with, if not also strong criticism of, the outcome of the referendum in the Greek Cypriot community.

What was actually regrettable was that Annan-V contained one-sided provisions that did not allow the majority community to endorse it. Outside parties appeared to want to close the book on Cyprus as quickly as possible so as to appease Turkey. The Greek Cypriots believe that, as the victims of invasion and occupation, they have to achieve a comprehensive, functional, and viable solution. This solution should stand the test of time and conform with European law and with the European Convention, as well as with the principles of the UN resolutions on Cyprus. Such a solution has to be perceived as fair by all the people who would have to live under it. Thus, no solution can succeed if it does not address the legitimate concerns that prevented the Greek Cypriots from approving Annan-V on 24 April 2004. Cosmetic changes to that plan will simply not suffice. The fact that Cyprus is a small and weak state makes it even more imperative that the solution should guarantee the enjoyment of fundamental rights that all other EU nationals enjoy under European law and the European Convention. Discrimination based on ethnicity or religion has no place in twenty-first-century Europe.

While some members of the international community were not familiar with the intricacies and weaknesses of Annan-V, the United States and Britain have attempted to use the outcome of the referendum to upgrade the regime of the occupied areas in an attempt to improve relations with Ankara. In doing so, they have used as a pretext Turkish Cypriot approval of Annan-V in the referendum of 24 April. They justify these actions on humanitarian grounds with the objective of "breaking the isolation of the Turkish Cypriots." The next section examines this argument and the fallacies surrounding it.

The Myth of the Turkish Cypriot "Isolation"

First, some comments about the political situation in the occupied areas and the attempt to upgrade the status of this illegal entity. The "TRNC" was illegal and remains illegal because of unanimous decisions by the UN Security Council,[1] the European Community, courts in Britain and the United States, and the European Court of Human Rights.[2] All court decisions reflect on the fact that the so-called "government" of the occupied areas is nothing more than a "subordinate local administration to Turkey." Approval by the Turkish Cypriots of Annan-V does not change this reality. The plan could not annul the aforementioned decisions and actions. Moreover, as he had indicated, unless his plan was approved by both communities, it was off the table. Members of the EU take pride in the fact that they have a community where law is supreme. Cyprus is an equal member of the EU and cannot be deprived of its rights and responsibilities in order to satisfy the interests of non-EU members. This would subvert the institutional integrity of the EU.

The United States and Britain, primarily, have shed crocodile tears about the isolation of the Turkish Cypriots and about the economic disparity between the occupied and the free areas of Cyprus. In order to appease Ankara, they conveniently lay the blame on the doorstep of the Greek Cypriots. But it was the Turkish invasion and continuing occupation of Cyprus that brought about the international actions leading to the ghetoization of the Turkish Cypriots; the economic disparity issue is real. The friends of Turkey should look at the consequences of Turkey's actions in Cyprus. Turkey brought in the settlers; Turkey introduced the Turkish lira in the occupied areas in 1983 and made it the official currency; Turkey brought in Turkish bureaucrats to manage the Turkish Cypriot economy. On numerous occasions during the 1980s and 90s, international financial institutions had to launch major rescue operations to save the Turkish economy from bankruptcy. Therefore, it is not surprising to see the economic disparity between the free and the occupied areas of the republic. Meanwhile, Annan-V absolved Turkey of all financial liability for its actions in Cyprus. Instead, it placed the economic burden of reunification on the Greek Cypriots and the international community.

With the connivance and tolerance of Turkey, since the demonstrations of January/February 2003 against the regime of Rauf Denktash, Washington has proceeded with another little-noticed regime change operation, this time in the occupied areas of Cyprus. By late spring of 2004, officials in Washington considered Denktash to be "in the dustbin of history" as "president" of an un-recognized state. In contrast, Mehmet Ali Talat was elevated and presented as "Mr. Prime Minister" and as the person who would lead the Turkish Cypriots into a new European era. However, Talat had been the so-called "prime minister" of the same unrecognized entity whose so-called "president" was Denktash. With Denktash's ignominious departure, Talat was elected "president" of the "TRNC."

Shedding crocodile tears about Turkish Cypriot isolation may serve Washington's regional strategic objectives but will not change the reality of the situation in the occupied areas. Any moves leading to the de facto recognition of the occupied area and its leadership will undermine regional stability, set a dangerous precedent for other regional problems such as that of Kosovo, and not lead to the reunification of Cyprus. Statements on behalf of Talat by the United States and Britain enhance Talat's intransigence and will destroy any semblance of objectivity for both countries in any future attempt to resolve the Cyprus Question. The same holds true for the United Nations. Echoing voices from Washington, former Cyprus negotiator Alvaro de Soto said that he cannot expect the Turkish Cypriots to renegotiate Annan-V once they accepted it without preconditions. With such an unrealistic outlook, can the United Nations remain an objective mediator in any future attempt to resolve the Cyprus Question? De Soto even went a step further when he said that the "Annan plan is there, there is no other plan," and that it was up to the Greek Cypriots to rethink their massive rejection of Annan-V.

Following consultations with the government of the Republic of Cyprus, the EU submitted a package of measures intended to bring the Turkish Cypriots closer to the EU and support the economic development of the occupied areas. As of the end of December 2005, these financial and trade measures had not been implemented because Turkey and the Turkish Cypriot leadership have attempted to use these measures for political gain leading to the de facto recognition of their illegal regime. The economic benefits package for the Turkish Cypriots has been sacrificed in a futile search for political gain.

Measures on Behalf of the Turkish Cypriots

Following the republic's accession to the EU, the government of Cyprus announced its own series of measures aiming to promote reunification and reconciliation. These confidence-building measures offer substantial tangible benefits to Turkish Cypriots who are citizens of the Republic of Cyprus. All these measures are in the context of the laws of the republic, the EU *acquis*, and international law. These measures include:[3]

- the movement of persons across the "green line" (the 1974 cease-fire line) including all EU citizens and third country nationals. Since the April 2003 lifting of many of the restrictions imposed by the Turkish Army on the freedom of movement of people, goods, and services across the cease-fire line, Greek Cypriots carried out an estimated 2.3 million visits to the occupied areas. Greek Cypriots visited their ancestral homes and various religious sites. In that two-year period, Greek Cypriots spent more than $57 million in the occupied areas during these visits.

- unmanning and removal of weaponry from military positions along the cease-fire line in Nicosia within the walls and in the Famagusta-Dehrynia area.

- refraining from certain types of military exercises along the buffer zone and within two kilometers of the cease-fire line.

- unilateral de-mining within the buffer zone in compliance with international conventions.

- the opening of additional crossing points to facilitate movement across the cease-fire line. However, the government of the republic has opposed any actions by the occupation authorities along the cease-fire line extending their control into the buffer zone. The Turkish forces have attempted to do that in the Ledra Street crossing in Nicosia within the walls, as well as in the buffer zone in Louroudjina and Strovilia.

- allowing free movement of public service vehicles owned by Turkish Cypriots to facilitate Turkish Cypriot trade and tourism.

- facilitating the movement of goods and services between the two communities.

- the employment of Turkish Cypriots in the free areas. As of April 2005, 2,659 Turkish Cypriots were registered with the Social Insurance Services (SIS). An additional 5,000 Turkish Cypriots are employed in the free areas without SIS registration. These workers have received an estimated $246 million in salaries over the last two years. These figures must be seen in the context of the size of the Turkish Cypriot community and the scale of its economy. In 2003 and 2004, Turkish Cypriots received some $43 million in social insurance pensions from government funds from the Republic of Cyprus.

- the issuance of official Republic of Cyprus documents to Turkish Cypriots entitled to them. By April 2005, 63,592 Turkish Cypriots acquired Republic of Cyprus birth certificates; 57,309 have acquired Republic of Cyprus identity cards; and 32,185 have acquired Republic of Cyprus passports. This is all the more impressive in view of the size of the Turkish Cypriot community and the fact that Turkish Cypriots were prohibited by the occupation authorities from possessing and using such documents. The occupation authorities do not recognize the Republic of Cyprus.

- the protection of the Turkish Cypriot cultural heritage. With funding from the state budget and support from the EU and UNOPS, Turkish Cypriot religious and other historic sites in the free areas have been renovated and maintained or are currently undergoing renovations. This is in sharp contrast with the systematic destruction of Orthodox churches and other Cypriot historical sites in the occupied areas.[4]

- health services. In the two-year period ending in April 2005, more than 24,000 Turkish Cypriots have been provided with quality free medical care at public hospitals and medical centers in the free areas of the Republic of Cyprus. The cost of treatment and medications exceeds $9 million. Turkish Cypriots are given priority medical care in these facilities.

- programming by the Cyprus Broadcasting Corporation has been upgraded to include more Turkish Cypriot programs.
- various forms of humanitarian assistance and cooperation.
- participation by Turkish Cypriots residing in the free areas of the republic in local and EU parliamentary elections.
- exports of Turkish Cypriot goods to the EU and third countries in accordance with the laws of the republic and the EU *acquis*.
- participation by Turkish Cypriots in EU research programs and in programs as Leonardo, Socrates, and the 6th framework.
- full tuition fees for Turkish Cypriot students attending private secondary schools in the free areas of the republic.
- utilities. Between 1974 and 1996, the Cyprus Electricity Authority provided free electricity to the occupied areas at a cost estimated at $343 million. During a major breakdown in the electrical grid of the occupied areas in January 2006, the Electricity Authority stepped in and, within hours, was able to provide electricity to the occupied area. This support lasted for over two weeks.

Despite obstacles by the occupation regime, especially in the implementation of EU trade regulations and financial assistance, these confidence-building measures are improving the economic situation of the Turkish Cypriots. Even though these measures are no substitute for a comprehensive solution to the Cyprus Question, they can contribute to a climate conducive to reconciliation and reunification.

Threats to Reunification and Reconciliation

As indicated earlier, following the outcome of the 24 April 2004 referenda, Turkey, the Turkish Cypriot leadership, and certain officials in the United States and Britain have sought ways to upgrade the status of the occupied areas, if not also to grant de facto recognition to the regime of the occupied areas. These actions have been justified as fulfilling the spirit of Annan-V, given its unconditional acceptance by the Turkish Cypriots. However, as Secretary-General Annan had indicated, the plan was "off the table" unless approved by both communities. The other argument in favor of these actions has been the lifting of the "isolation" of the Turkish Cypriots. This myth has already been explored and exposed earlier in this chapter.

These actions have taken the form of invitations extended to Turkish Cypriot leader Mehmet Ali Talat to visit Washington, New York, and London. Similar was the visit and meeting by British foreign secretary Jack Straw with Talat on 25 January 2006 in the occupied areas. The meeting was held in the office of the so-called president of the unrecognized "TRNC" with all appropriate insignia and symbols in display. Even though these invitations and meetings have been extended to Talat as leader of the Turkish Cypriot community, the media in the occupied areas have presented these invitations and meetings as official diplomatic functions implying de facto recognition. Similarly presented were visits by a few members of the U.S. House of Representatives, some Congressional staff members, and a small U.S. business delegation to the occupied areas. The visits that took place in the spring and summer of 2005 were orchestrated by Turkish-American organizations with the cooperation of the U.S. embassy in Nicosia. These individuals entered Cyprus via the illegal and internationally unauthorized Tymbou Airport. With great fanfare from the Turkish Cypriot media, these isolated actions were presented as putting an end to Turkish Cypriot isolation and providing de facto recognition. Such largely symbolic actions are making reunification harder by increasing Turkish Cypriot intransigence.

The risk of furthering divisions in Cyprus is evidenced by three other more dangerous scenarios that have been presented under the guise of ending the Turkish Cypriot isolation. None of these scenarios involve the de jure recognition of the "TRNC." However, all three scenarios have serious legal, political, and economic consequences that are likely to make any future attempt at reunification even harder.

The first scenario considers the illegal "TRNC" as an "autonomous entity of the EU." This is the so-called Emerson Model of the Brussels-based Centre for European Policy Studies. In their view, because of decisions by the UN Security Council and other international and regional organizations, the "TRNC" remains part of the Republic of Cyprus but not under the control of the government of the republic. The "TRNC," through "democratic and legitimate procedures," is a self-governing entity, enjoying autonomy. It is able to adopt its own legislation and has the ability to harmonize its laws with European legislation. Thus, the so-called "TRNC" is an "autonomous territory of the EU" and can be treated as such in trade and other political matters. Similar ideas have been promoted in a study by Dov Lynch for the U.S. Institute for Peace, a think tank of the U.S. Department of State. Elements of this proposal found their way into the 24 January 2006 proposals by Turkish prime minister Recep Tayyip Erdogan on the resolution of the Cyprus Question.

Turkey and the Turkish Cypriot leadership with U.S. and British support have attempted to implement this model, capitalizing on a confidence-building decision made jointly by the EU Commission and the government of the Republic of Cyprus on 7 July 2004. That decision entailed a two-year economic development package for the Turkish Cypriots worth 259 million euros, along with provisions on trade from the occupied areas to the EU and across the cease-fire line. Half of the aid funding expired at the end of 2005 because of unacceptable Turkish and Turkish Cypriot demands to link aid and trade to the opening of Turkish Cypriot ports and airports. The Turkish Cypriots and Britain attempted to implement the Emerson Model by insisting that the commission extend trade privileges to the Turkish Cypriots under Article 133 of the EU Treaty. This article covers trade with "third countries" and territories. This clear attempt at de facto recognition of the autonomy of the "TRNC" failed. On 24 February 2006, the Austrian presidency of the EU announced that the COREPER meeting decided that trade with the occupied areas must conform to the terms of Protocol 10 of the Cyprus Accession Treaty. That treaty recognizes only the Republic of Cyprus as the sole subject of international law. Any decisions under the protocol require unanimity of all EU member states. Thus, the legitimate government of the Republic of Cyprus cannot be bypassed with a trade ruling that may result in the de facto recognition of an illegal political entity.

The second and more dangerous scenario is that of the Taiwan Model. In discussing this scenario, it should be noted that the "TRNC" is the result of an illegal invasion, occupation, and secession of portions of the internationally recognized Republic of Cyprus. International courts and all international and regional organizations consider the formation of the "TRNC" to be illegal. Successive decisions by the European Court of Human Rights find the authorities of the occupied areas to be "a subordinate local administration to Turkey." In contrast, Taiwan exists because of an inconclusive civil war. Until recently, each of the governments based in Beijing and Taipei claimed that there is one China with one government. Thus, in the case of Taiwan, the challenge for the international community was which of the two governments was the legitimate government of China. This issue was settled in 1971 when the People's Republic of China won the argument. Since then, the shadowy status of Taiwan has been the source of global diplomatic and political friction. The threat of regional instability and conflict also exists if Taiwan persists in its quest for independence and recognition. Taiwan has utilized its economic strength and ties with conservative American political circles to maintain its shadowy existence, while the international community continues to press both sides for a peaceful reunification of Taiwan to China, under a special status recognizing its unique cultural, social, economic, and political characteristics.

The Republic of Cyprus maintains full diplomatic relations with Beijing. However, because of international trade agreements under the General Agreement on Tariffs and Trade (GATT) and the World Trade Organization (WTO) dating to earlier times, Taiwan is considered a "separate customs territory." Taiwan was a founding member of GATT and its agreements have been incorporated into the WTO that China just recently joined. Under the rules of the WTO, Taiwan, since January 2002, is known as "Chinese Taipei" and is part of the so-called "separate customs territory of Taiwan, Pengpu, Kinmen an Matsu." This issue becomes even more complicated because Hong Kong and Macao, on the basis of being at one time overseas territories of England and Portugal, respectively, came under the GATT agreement in 1981 and 1991. They are currently known as Hong Kong-China and Macao-China. Taiwan is not a member of any international organization other than the WTO. Taiwan participates in the affairs of the Asian Development Bank and the Asian-Pacific Economic Cooperation Group. Any attempt to grant a "Taiwan" status to the "TRNC" will violate international decisions on the status of this entity. It will also contribute to the permanent division of Cyprus and to regional instability.

The third scenario is that of the "Kosovo Free Trade Area." This is another troubling precedent for the situation in Cyprus. On 7 July 2003, Albania and the UN Interim Administration in Kosovo, on behalf of the provisional institutions of Kosovo's self-governing authority, concluded a free trade agreement. Albania is a member of the WTO. Serbia/Montenegro has WTO observer status. For the time, Kosovo remains an autonomous province of Serbia not currently under the control of the government of Serbia/Montenegro. Even though at this time the Albanian-Kosovar agreement has not been ratified by the WTO, the precedent it creates may be even more difficult than the case of Taiwan. It simply provides a more flexible formula for economic relations with another shadowy entity whose status has yet to be finalized. This precedent, along with the other two scenarios outlined in this section, will contribute neither to reconciliation nor to reunification in Cyprus. Actions enhancing the autonomy of the occupied areas will further enhance the negotiating intransigence of the Turkish Cypriot leadership and Turkey. Such steps will likely lead to partition rather than reunification.

The three scenarios outlined in this section are not the result of the 24 April 2004 "no" vote on Annan-V by the Greek Cypriots. The Greek Cypriot vote has been used as an excuse to meet Turkey's objectives. It should be noted that, had Annan-V been approved by the Greek Cypriot community, these scenarios would have been equally plausible. Under the Annan plan, the component states of the new republic would have the right to legally engage in their own international economic activities with minimal, if any, central supervision. Under the confederation promoted by the Annan plan these activities would have been forerunners of Turkish Cypriot independence, especially if there were difficulties in the implementation of Annan-V.

In conclusion, these rumored actions can have only one effect. They will perpetuate the division of Cyprus. As indicated in this chapter, this is not an acceptable option.

Turkey and the European Union

With the support of the Republic of Cyprus, the European Council on 17 December 2004, invited Turkey to open accession talks with the EU on 3 October 2005. It should be noted that under the Annan plan Cyprus would have been obligated to support Turkey's European aspirations. This was another attempt to limit the sovereign rights of the Republic of Cyprus. In the discussions leading to the European Council decisions on Turkey's candidacy both in December 2004 and in September/October 2005, the Republic of Cyprus made a deliberate decision to endorse Turkey's application. The reason for this decision was the belief that Turkey's accession path would likely encourage conduct contributing to democratization in Turkey, the respect of human rights in the country, and peace and security in Cyprus.

Leading EU members such as France and Austria had serious concerns about Turkey's application and potential EU accession. This was evident in the European Council debates prior to the 3 October 2005 EU decision to start accession negotiations with Turkey. This particularly sensitive issue had a major effect in the rejection of the European Constitution in the referenda held in France and in the Netherlands earlier in the year. Cyprus did not succumb to domestic and external pressures to cast a veto on Turkey's application. The veto was a power available to all EU members.

Cyprus, along with other EU members, worked hard to attain certain commitments on the part of the EU and Turkey as to Turkey's obligations vis-à-vis Cyprus despite British opposition. Turkey, however, has not reciprocated. In a blunt and defiant manner, on 28 March 2005 Turkey initialed the Draft Protocol regarding the adaptation of the Ankara Agreement to the ten new EU member states. It also declared that its action did not amount to the recognition of the Republic of Cyprus, or to its "de-recognition" of the "Turkish Republic of Northern Cyprus." It also maintained that Turkish ports, airports, and air corridors would remain closed to Cypriot vessels and aircraft. The next day, the commission spokesman noted that this was a violation of the Customs Union Agreement between the EU and Turkey.

Turkey's behavior has been unprecedented. No previous EU applicant state has failed to recognize an EU member. No other EU applicant state has ever relied on threats and negative allegations against the EU in order to obtain a date for accession talks. In case the EU failed to grant such a date, Turkey accused the EU of being a "Christian Club" discriminating against a Muslim country. At the same time, Turkey questioned EU demands for full compliance with the Copenhagen criteria in view of Turkey's different culture, customs, and traditions. This is somewhat ironic, in view of Turkish allegations of European discrimination when EU political leaders and media pointed to Turkey's different culture and its incompatibility to European norms. Turkey also demanded that it would accept full membership and not a special status short of full membership.

On 21 September 2005, the EU Commission formally responded to Turkey's declarations at the time of the actual signing of the Additional Protocol to the Ankara Agreement.[5] In paragraph 1 of this declaration, the EU expressed its regret that Turkey made this declaration on Cyprus. It went on to say that the EU considered this declaration to be unilateral and therefore having no effect on Turkey's obligations under the Protocol. Paragraph 3 of the EU response clearly stated that Turkey's compliance will be monitored for full implementation during 2006 and that failure to implement its obligations in full will affect the overall progress in the EU/Turkey negotiations. More importantly, paragraph 4 of this declaration stated in unqualified terms that the Republic of Cyprus became an EU member on 1 May 2004, and the EU recognizes only the Republic of Cyprus as a subject of international law. The declaration went on to say that recognition of all EU members is a necessary component of the accession process and called on Turkey to normalize its relations with all EU members as soon as possible. The European Council declared its intention to monitor the progress made on all issues in 2006. It also endorsed the efforts of the secretary-general to bring about a comprehensive settlement on Cyprus in line with the UN Security Council resolutions and the principles on which the EU is founded. These EU warnings have also been repeated by Oli Rehn, the EU commissioner responsible for enlargement.

On 3 October 2005, the EU Intergovernmental Conference invited Turkey to open accession negotiations. In the ceremony that followed the lengthy and rancorous negotiations about Turkey's accession and the form such accession might take, the EU presented two major documents.[6] The first was the Opening Statement for the Accession Conference with Turkey which reminded that the European Economic Community (EEC) and Turkey signed in 1963 an Association Agreement, known as the Ankara Agreement.

In 1987, Turkey formally applied for membership in the EEC. Turkey's relations with the EEC/EU were expanded in 1995 with the signing of the Customs Union Agreement. Finally, in 1999, at the Helsinki European Council meeting, Turkey was granted candidate status. The opening statement reiterated the council's 21 September 2005 statement discussed earlier in this chapter. It also recalled the significance and the nature of the accession process and reminded Turkey that the EU's Intergovernmental Conference involves all EU members and that decisions are taken on the basis of unanimity. That was a clear but indirect inference that Cyprus as an EU member did have the right of veto. The opening statement also covered the need for the continuation and implementation of the required domestic reforms in Turkey.

The second and lengthier document involved the negotiating framework and included the principles and procedures governing the negotiations. This important document included, among others, the following principles:

- Negotiations based on Turkey's own merits and progress in meeting membership requirements.
- Accession as the shared objective of the negotiations. However, the negotiations involve an open-ended process, the outcome of which cannot be guaranteed. In addition to fulfilling the Copenhagen criteria, the EU will also take into account its absorption capacity. This was a most significant point intended to allay the fears of many members about the impact on the EU of a developing country with a population of more than 70 million.
- Full implementation of the Copenhagen criteria which have been enshrined in article 6(1) of the EU Treaty and in the Charter of Fundamental Rights.
- Suspension of the negotiations upon breach of these criteria.
- Turkey's unequivocal commitment to good neighborly relations and its undertaking to resolve any outstanding border disputes in accordance with the UN Charter and, if necessary, with resort to the International Court of Justice. This was a clear, even though indirect, reference to Turkey's problems with Greece and Cyprus.
- Turkey's continued efforts to achieve a comprehensive settlement of the Cyprus Question within the UN framework and in line with the principles on which the EU is founded.
- Normalization of relations with the Republic of Cyprus.
- Fulfillment of Turkey's obligations under the Association Agreement and under the Additional Protocol. This was another indirect reference to Turkey's nonimplementation of its obligations vis-à-vis Cyprus.
- Close monitoring by the commission of Turkey's compliance in all areas of the negotiations.

There were additional principles included in these documents. What has been included here primarily reflects the position of the EU on the Cyprus Question. However much Turkey may wish to avoid this issue with meaningless unilateral declarations and actions, the EU does not plan to and must not let Turkey off the hook. The current awkward and anomalous situation where an EU candidate state refuses to recognize one of the EU members which will be voting on Turkey's accession will need to be rectified soon. For its part, the Republic of Cyprus has done its best on the issue of Turkey's accession process and cannot be accused of obstructionism. Now, the ball is in Turkey's court. Meaningless public relations gestures, such as the "plan" announced by Turkish prime minister Erdogan on 24 January 2006, will neither resolve the Cyprus Question nor free Turkey of its EU obligations vis-à-vis the Republic of Cyprus.

In closing, the reader may have noticed critical comments regarding the role of the United States and Britain in the case of Cyprus, especially in the 1999–2004 cycle of negotiations and in the aftermath of the 24 April 2004 referenda. It is worth noting that the United States, a non-EU member, has lobbied the EU hard on behalf of Turkey's accession and has attempted not only to link Turkey's accession to that of Cyprus, but also to make the resolution of the Cyprus Question a prerequisite of Cypriot accession. The United States was unsuccessful in this gambit. Had it been successful, the Cypriot application would have been hostage to Turkey's demands and policies. American lobbying on behalf of Turkey in the EU reached its apex at the November 2002 Copenhagen EU Council meeting. Even friends of the United States advised Washington that its lobbying served neither Turkey's interests nor the relations of the EU with the United States.

Great Britain presided over the EU in the second half of 2005. It, too, went beyond acceptable limits in drafting the October 2005 accession documents analyzed earlier in this chapter. The first drafts of these documents avoided the critical issues involving Turkey's accession and had no references in regard to Turkey's obligations on Cyprus. It was only after lengthy negotiations involving not only Cyprus but also countries like France, Austria, Spain, and others that a deadlock was avoided and the accession talks with Turkey convened on 3 October 2005. The American and British actions in regard to Turkey's EU case were characteristic examples of the motives that guided their policies on Cyprus during the negotiations on the Annan plan.

At the time of this writing, the EU and Turkey are engaged in a technical screening of Turkish legislation relating to the thirty-two chapters that make up the foundation of the accession talks. As the documents of 3 October 2005 indicate, the accession process is open ended. If full membership were to be granted to Turkey, this would not take place for at least fifteen years. In addition to the conditional wording in the accession statements, Turkey's case will be affected by the future direction of the European Union and its constitution, along with the state of European politics and economy fifteen years from now.

The UN, the EU, and a European Solution to the Cyprus Question

In May 2005, Tassos Tzionis, personal envoy of the president of the Republic of Cyprus, met with the UN under-secretary-general for political affairs, Sir Kieran Prendergast, in New York. In several meetings they reviewed the views of the government of the Republic of Cyprus on both the procedure and the substance of any future talks under the good offices mission of the secretary-general. A year had passed since the referendum of 24 April 2004 and the accession of Cyprus to the EU. This year-long period provided an adequate cooling-off time for all sides to reassess the past, and to evaluate the conditions created by the accession of Cyprus to the EU and the anticipated accession talks between the EU and Turkey.

Following these meetings, Prendergast visited Cyprus, Greece, and Turkey between 30 May and 7 June 2005 for further consultations. Reporting to the Security Council, the undersecretary indicated that it would be "prudent to proceed very carefully" and that the secretary-general "intends to reflect on the mission of good offices in the period ahead." It was apparent that no common ground existed in order to enable the resumption of a new round of negotiations. The president of the Republic of Cyprus also met with the secretary-general in New York on 16 September 2005 during the opening session of the General Assembly to review the conditions for a renewed UN initiative on Cyprus.

The Greek Cypriot position is very clear. Any future talks will be held under the auspices of the good offices mission of the secretary-general as originally conceived and not as unilaterally altered in the 2004 round of the talks. This means that arbitration, tight negotiating deadlines amounting to an ultimatum, and an agreement that has not been negotiated and mutually accepted by the parties will not be part of any future UN-sponsored talks. While the fundamental parameters of the Annan plan provide the negotiating framework, the new talks will account for the legitimate concerns of the Greek Cypriots that led to their overwhelming rejection of Annan-V. Simply put, cosmetic changes to Annan-V will not suffice. Even though a new round of talks will be under the auspices of the UN, the talks reflect the fact that Cyprus is a member of the EU. Outside parties cannot play the role they did during the 2004 talks, nor can they relegate the EU to an observer status as they did at Burgenstock in March 2004. A new round of talks must be based not only on the UN Security Council resolutions on Cyprus, but also on EU law and the various court decisions on Cyprus. Cypriots cannot accept derogations from EU laws that will make them second-class citizens in the EU and in their own country.

This is why, increasingly, we hear the term a "European solution" to the Cyprus Question. As indicated, this does not imply bypassing UN procedures for the pacific settlement of disputes. What the term does imply is that the UN, in its peacemaking role, must base its actions on standards conforming with the European reality and with the fact that Cyprus is an EU member with all the rights and responsibilities of membership, while Turkey aspires to become a member.

What is meant by a "European solution"?

- A solution based on the principles on which the EU is founded. That means freedom, democracy, the rule of law within and among states, human rights, and nondiscrimination on the basis of ethnic origin or religion. Implementation of these principles excludes provisions in Annan-V that discriminated on the basis of ethnicity and religion.
- Opposing provisions such as those providing for foreign occupation armies with intervention rights as proposed in Annan-V.
- Implying free choice in electoral procedures with the right to elect and to be elected and equal access regardless of ethnicity or religion.
- Upholding the rights of the displaced to their homes and properties. At the end of the day, the European Convention and its Protocols are the foundation of European democracy.

That is what a "European solution" for Cyprus is all about, and this is what Annan-V failed to provide. This is why Kofi Annan and his supporters fought so hard to have a settlement that violated all these provisions concluded before the 1 May 2004 accession of Cyprus to the EU. This is the new reality facing the United Nations, the EU, Cyprus, and Turkey, and all other interested outside parties.

CHAPTER FIVE

Cyprus and the European Union

ON 1 MAY 2004 Cyprus joined the European Union. This was a landmark event in the long history of Cyprus. It also marked the fulfillment of a major objective of successive Cypriot governments. EU membership was a natural choice for Cyprus, which had been part of Europe in terms of history, civilization, culture, and economic ties. Moreover, it shared with Western Europe a commitment to democracy, the rule of law, human rights, and freedoms. This is why Cyprus, soon after independence, became a signatory of the European Convention on Human Rights and a member of the Council of Europe. In 1975, Cyprus also became a member of the Organization for Security and Cooperation in Europe (OSCE).

A Brief Chronology

Economic motives led the Republic of Cyprus in 1971 to enter into negotiations with the EEC. On 19 December 1972, Cyprus and the EEC signed an Association Agreement aiming to establish, in two stages and over a ten-year period, a Customs Union Agreement. The implementation of the Association Agreement was interrupted by the 1974 Turkish invasion of Cyprus. The invasion and the occupation of nearly 37 percent of the republic's territory and the forcible movement of nearly half of the population of the republic disrupted the Cypriot economy and created major dislocations in all economic sectors. This is why the second stage of the Association Agreement did not come into force until 1 January 1988, while the Customs Union was envisioned to come into effect by 2003 at the latest.

While the EEC and Cyprus developed their economic association, the EEC/EU itself was undertaking major steps leading to its own economic and political integration. There was growing political consensus in the free areas of the republic that Cyprus ought to contribute to and benefit from the emerging European integration. On 4 July 1990, Cyprus formally applied for membership in the EEC. The application was submitted under article 49 of the EEC Treaty. On 30 June 1994, the Commission of the European Communities issued its "Avis" (opinion) on the Cypriot application.[1] The positive opinion reflected on the cultural, political, historical, and economic bonds common between the EEC and Cyprus. It also concluded that the accession of Cyprus would increase security and prosperity on the island and contribute to reconciliation among the two communities. The commission was aware of the political and economic obstacles created by the division of the island and addressed the need for a "peaceful, balanced and lasting settlement of the Cyprus Question" which would allow Cyprus to participate in the community's decision making and apply correctly community law throughout the island.

The commission's opinion that declared the Republic of Cyprus eligible for membership was welcomed at the Brussels meeting of the council on 19 and 20 July 1993. The opinion was affirmed at the Luxembourg meeting of the council on 4 October 1993. The council also invited the commission to enter into substantive discussions with the government of Cyprus to help it prepare for the accession negotiations; pledged its support to the secretary-general's efforts to produce a political settlement of the Cyprus Question; and agreed to evaluate the accession process in the context of such a settlement.

At its Corfu meeting on 24 and 25 June 1994, the European Council confirmed that Cyprus and Malta would be part of the next enlargement of the European Union. A few months later, on 6 March 1995, the EU General Affairs Council reaffirmed the eligibility of Cyprus for membership and stipulated that accession negotiations with Cyprus would start six months after the conclusion of the 1996 EU Intergovernmental Conference.

On 15 July 1997, the commission issued another important document on the challenge of enlargement known as "Agenda 2000."[2] Noting the "advanced level of development and economic dynamism" of Cyprus, the EU Commission concluded that accession negotiations could start before a political settlement was reached and that, if the question had not been resolved before negotiations were due to begin, "they should be opened with the government of the Republic of Cyprus, as the only authority recognized by international law." This important statement recognized that in postinvasion Cyprus there was only one legitimate state and government. This was important in order to keep Cyprus from becoming hostage to Turkish policy. This point will be developed further later in this chapter.

True to its word, the commission opened accession negotiations with the Republic of Cyprus on 31 March 1998. As in all membership applications, the process started with a screening of the *acquis* and of Cypriot legislation to identify areas requiring harmonization with EU laws and institutions. It was followed by substantive negotiations on all twenty-nine chapters required by EU accession procedures. Cyprus was the first among the ten countries involved in this EU enlargement phase to complete its negotiations. It did so by December 2002.

At the historic EU Copenhagen meeting on 12 and 13 December 2002,[3] the European Council decided to admit Cyprus to the EU along with nine other candidate states. The Treaty of Accession for the new members was signed in Athens, Greece, on 16 April 2003 and came into force on 1 May 2004. It is important to note that it was the Republic of Cyprus as created in 1960 that was admitted to the EU and that the signatory of the Accession Treaty was the internationally recognized government of the Republic of Cyprus. This reflected the consistent EU policy that, despite the division brought about by the 1974 Turkish invasion, the EU recognized the territorial integrity and sovereignty of the Republic of Cyprus and the legitimacy of its government. The government represented all Cypriots. In view of the continuing division of Cyprus, a protocol was annexed to the Accession Treaty providing for the suspension of the *acquis* in the Turkish-occupied areas of the republic. At the same time, the EU decided that it was ready to accommodate the terms of a future settlement "in line with the principles on which the EU is founded." This statement became an object of controversy when Secretary-General Kofi Annan sought the adoption into EU primary law of the derogations contained in Annan-V prior to the accession of Cyprus to the EU. While the secretary-general relied on the EU's willingness to "accommodate the terms of a future settlement," the government of Cyprus insisted that this accommodation had to conform to "the principles on which the EU is founded." As shown, for the Greek Cypriots, Annan-V failed that test.

Obstacles on the Road to Brussels

Early on in its application process, Cyprus fully met the Copenhagen criteria for membership in the EU.[4] However, its application process was affected by various problems. One was the philosophical debate within the EU on the "widening" and the "deepening" of the EU.[5] The "widening" debate involved cultural, political, and economic issues, as well as the effect of new members on the institutional cohesion and political direction of the EU.

Two prospective applicants, Cyprus and Malta, were Mediterranean mini-states. Countries like Germany at first favored only an Eastern European expansion. Others, like France, Italy, and Greece, believed that enlargement could not come about without a Mediterranean dimension. By the time of the EU Council meetings in Corfu and Essen (24–25 June and 9–10 December 1994) that issue had been largely resolved. The council declared that Malta and Cyprus would be included in the next round of EU enlargement.

Another problem was specific to Cyprus. It had to do with the lack of resolution of the Cyprus Question. Could a divided Cyprus enter the EU? Would the accession process influence the on-going, but often stalemated, negotiations under the good offices of the secretary-general? If so, how? How was Turkey's European quest affected by Turkey's continuing occupation, by the stalemated Cyprus talks, and by the Cypriot application to the EU? How did influential members of the EU like Britain, and non-EU members like the United States, respond to the Cypriot accession case? These questions will be discussed below. First, however, a general assessment of why the accession of Cyprus was of interest to the EU.

In contrast to other candidate states, Cyprus easily fulfilled the economic and political/legal criteria for EU membership. Moreover, harmonization had already been well under way as Cyprus entered in the first phase of its Customs Union with the EU. Cyprus's geographic position was a major asset, being at the crossroads of transport and communication routes linking Europe to the Middle East and Central Asia. Cyprus had skilled human resources, an advanced technical infrastructure, and one of the largest commercial fleets in the world. Working with other EU member states and institutions, Cyprus could contribute to common problem areas involving illicit migration, money laundering, narcotics control, human trafficking, environmental issues, and even the threat of terrorism. Thus, the inclusion of Cyprus and Malta met the EU objectives in the Mediterranean.

New EU candidacies, including that of Cyprus, were handled by the legal and political institutions of the EU (Council and Commission) and by the European Parliament. Cypriot diplomats and technocrats in the negotiating team faced a demanding multidimensional task. They met the challenge successfully and ahead of all other candidate states.[6] Cyprus was aware that, in contrast to the candidacies of the nine other applicant states, the Cypriot case hinged on the political issue of a resolution of the Cyprus Question. Cyprus had the goodwill and the commitment to resolve the question within the clear legal and political parameters already discussed. The question, however, was complicated by external factors, that is, the interests and policies of influential states such as the United States and Britain. These states defined their Cyprus policy in the context of their policy toward Turkey and their broader regional strategic needs. Thus, for Cyprus, the challenge was to have its accession not become a case of political football. The bottom line for Cyprus was that accession was different from a resolution of the Cyprus Question. Successive Cypriot governments argued that EU accession opened new opportunities for a resolution of this long-standing problem of invasion, occupation, and violation of human rights.

The Cypriot Strategy

The political dimensions of Cypriot accession strategy focused on the following goals:

- Developing a domestic political consensus on the accession of Cyprus to the EU. Throughout the 1980s there had been serious ideological opposition to accession by AKEL, the Communist Party of Cyprus. The end of the Cold War and the realization of the long-term political and economic benefits of accession brought about a pragmatic change in AKEL's position. Thus, when Cyprus formally applied for membership it did so with a broad political consensus.
- Avoiding the linkage of the Cypriot application to that of Turkey. Each application was separate and had to be judged on its own merits. This position was in response to Anglo-American efforts to link the two applications for maximum leverage on Cyprus and on the EU. Otherwise, the Cypriot application would be held hostage by Turkey, which could delay a resolution of the question until the EU responded positively to the Turkish accession case.
- Gaining support for the previously stated goals by key EU members such as France, Germany, Italy, and the United Kingdom.

- Assuring full cooperation and coordination with Greece, which was an EU member. Greece could influence, if not also control, the future expansion of the EU in view of the unanimity requirement for the addition of new members. Had the Cypriot accession case stalled because of failure to resolve the Cyprus Question, none of the other nine applicant members could expect accession to the EU. As it will become apparent from the discussion in this chapter, the Cypriot strategy fully met its goals.

The architect of the definition and coordination of Cypriot and Greek policy was the late Greek deputy foreign minister Yannos Kranidiotis, himself of Cypriot origin.[7] He ardently believed that:

- Cyprus's accession to the EU was separate from a resolution of the political question.
- Accession would encourage a resolution of the question by providing new options for addressing long-standing issues.
- Greece should lift its veto on the EU Financial Protocol on Turkey, if Turkey would commit to a legitimate process for a resolution of Greek-Turkish differences.
- Turkey should be granted EU candidate status with a clear road map of obligations. Included in these obligations would be a resolution of Greek-Turkish problems and to the Cyprus Question.

It was in the context of Kranidiotis's policy that Greece lifted its veto on Turkey's EU Financial Protocol in 1995. Further, on 10–11 December 1999 in Helsinki, the EU opened the way to Turkey's candidacy, even though it did not grant a date for commencing accession talks. The latter action came with the clear road map previously outlined. For Cyprus, however, the Helsinki EU Summit affirmed a key goal of Cypriot policy. Paragraph 9b of the Presidency Conclusions stated that:

> The European Council underlines that a political settlement will facilitate the accession of Cyprus to the European Union. If no settlement has been reached by the completion of accession negotiations, the Council's decision on accession will be made without the above being a precondition. In this the Council will take into account all relevant factors.[8]

Although the last sentence of the Helsinki Declaration was intended to accommodate British concerns about a divided Cyprus entering the EU, for all practical purposes the EU Council had removed the main obstacle to the accession of Cyprus. The Republic of Cyprus would not be held hostage to Turkish policy on Cyprus. This was a setback for Anglo-American policy which, as it will be shown later in the chapter, sought to link the Turkish EU accession process and the resolution of the Cyprus Question with the Cypriot application for EU accession. It took the personal intervention of President Clinton and other EU officials with Turkish prime minister Bulent Ecevit to gain his acceptance of the Helsinki formula. Turkey had been unhappy with the negative 1997 Luxembourg decision on its EU candidacy. And two years later, Turkey was unhappy that even though it had received EU candidate status, there were conditions attached on Cyprus and on the resolution of Greek-Turkish differences. This was a classic Turkish negotiating tactic. No other EU candidate state had to be coaxed to accept behavior compatible with international standards.

Economic motives brought about the association of Cyprus to the EEC in 1972. Over time, the political objectives of accession gained preeminence in Cypriot strategy. EU accession became the main foreign policy objective of all Cypriot governments starting late in the 1980s. There were many reasons for this choice, including the lack of progress in the negotiations on the Cyprus Question, the failure of the United Nations to implement the unanimous Security Council resolutions on Cyprus, and the pro-Turkish tilt of Anglo-American policy. Thus, the Cypriot political objectives included:

- Consolidating and strengthening Cypriot ties to Western European institutions, processes, and policies. This became an important goal following the end of the Cold War. Until then, Cyprus had been a leader in the Nonaligned Movement, while Turkey cooperated closely with NATO and the United States.
- Confirming the independence, sovereignty, and territorial integrity of Cyprus. The EEC, like other regional and international organizations and the rest of the international community, did not recognize the "Turkish Republic of Northern Cyprus" that was created in 1983 under the auspices of the Turkish occupation forces. Despite Turkish objections,[9] the Republic of Cyprus as created in 1960 was treated as a sovereign entity and its government was considered as the sole legitimate authority on the island. In addition, the European Parliament, through repeated resolutions, endorsed the independence, sovereignty, and territorial integrity of Cyprus and promoted the cause of human rights on the island.
- Increasing Cyprus's international bargaining power. Through solidarity, coalitions, and alliances with other EU members, Cyprus could counter more effectively Turkey's hegemonic ambitions, especially at a time when Turkey aspired to become an EU member. Turkey's EU case was supported primarily by the United States and Great Britain. The same two countries promoted Turkey's claims through the United Nations and the good offices of the secretary-general.
- Lessening external interference and defusing attempts at imposing solutions not serving Cypriot interests. This became a pressing priority after 1999 and the new Anglo-American initiatives that led to the presentation of the five versions of the Annan plan.
- Assisting in the resolution of the Cyprus Question. EU law and the European Convention could provide new solutions to issues of human rights that had plagued the negotiations until then. The same was true on security-related issues.
- Completing needed internal reforms and developing new foreign policy directions, as with the Common Foreign and Security Policy

(CFSP) and the EPC (European Political Cooperation). Changes in these policy areas were often opposed by parties such as AKEL. Since accession, such policy changes could be rationalized in the context of the europeanization of Cypriot foreign and security policy.

These political goals were not unrealistic. Cypriot policy elites were aware of the limitations of the emerging EU institutions, especially in the areas of foreign and security policy. This became apparent when issues of EU/NATO security cooperation were discussed. In the 12 December 2002 Copenhagen meeting, the EU Council agreed that the "Berlin Plus" security cooperation applied only to those EU member states which were either members of NATO or of the Partnership for Peace (PFP), or which had concluded bilateral security agreements with NATO. This clearly excluded Cyprus, which, because of American, British, and Turkish objections, could not become a member of either NATO or the PFP. However, the same declaration made it clear that all EU members participate fully in the definition and implementation of EU's Common Foreign and Security Policy.[10] This was a very important element for Cyprus because it opposed the secretary-general's attempt in Annan-V to exclude Cyprus from European security and foreign policy planning and to commit itself to offering open-ended support for Turkey's EU aspirations, regardless of whether Turkey met the Copenhagen criteria.

The Turkish and American Response to the Cyprus EU Application

Following the Commission's opinion of 30 June 1993 in favor of the candidacy of Cyprus for EU membership, the United States began reevaluating its policy on the European involvement in the Cyprus Question. The U.S. Department of State representative in Cyprus, Ambassador Nelson Ledsky, had steadfastly opposed any European involvement. His reasons included:

- his low regard for the community's effectiveness in addressing foreign policy problems;
- the EU's lack of interest in Turkey's European aspirations;
- the divergence of European and American foreign and security policy goals, especially because of France's influence; and
- the fact that the Cyprus Question was in the domain of the UN.

The Cyprus Question was of primary concern to American foreign policy because of its impact on Greco-Turkish relations and on NATO's cohesion and effectiveness. The architect of the new American approach to Cyprus was Ambassador Richard Holbrooke. Under his influence, during the second term of the Clinton administration the United States endorsed the membership of Cyprus in the EU. However, U.S. motives were not pure. Through this policy change Washington sought "to kill two birds with one stone." Supporting the case of Cyprus for EU accession could become a new source of leverage on Cyprus. By linking accession to the solution of the Cyprus Question, Cyprus could not refuse participation in UN/U.S. sponsored talks. It would also be

pressed to show flexibility and goodwill toward UN/U.S. proposals for the resolution of the Cyprus Question. Unless Cyprus made the needed concessions
demanded by Turkey, it could be accused of intransigence and jeopardize its
EU accession prospects.

At the same time, the United States would strengthen its relations with
Turkey by being its main advocate for EU accession, lobbying on behalf of
Turkey among EU members, and insisting on parallel progress in the Turkish
and the Cypriot applications. It was rather ironic that the United States, a non-
EU member, lobbied so hard on behalf of a prospective EU applicant.
Washington derived all the political benefit from its advocacy of Ankara's case
without having to bear any of the political, legal, and economic costs of
Turkey's EU membership.

The linkage of the resolution of the Cyprus Question to the accession
of Cyprus to the EU facilitated Turkey's case in Europe by removing the question as an obstacle to Turkey's European aspirations. Washington clearly understood that unless the question was resolved, Turkey would find it difficult to
make progress in its EU case. Rather than pressing Turkey, it was easier to
seek concessions from the Greek Cypriots in order to arrive at a solution.
Alvaro de Soto, the secretary-general's chief negotiator in the critical talks from
1999–2004, shared Washington's views. Consequently, de Soto, Ambassador
Tom Weston, and Lord David Hannay coordinated their tactics and objectives
with the clear aim of having the comprehensive UN plan, with all its derogations from EU law, approved prior to the accession of Cyprus to the EU.
Washington's lobbying on behalf of Turkey reached its climax at the December
2002 Copenhagen EU Council meeting. Even EU friends of the United States
were disturbed by Washington's high-handed lobbying tactics. The United
States continued its pro-Turkish EU policy, with support from de Soto, by in-
corporating in the various versions of the Annan plan provisions committing
Cyprus to provide open-ended support to Turkey's EU aspirations regardless
of whether Turkey met the EU membership criteria.

The case of the purchase and deployment of the Russian S-300 defensive anti-aircraft missile system by the Republic of Cyprus during 1997 and
1998, years critical to the Cypriot case in the EU, provided an unexpected
means of pressure in the hands of the United States. Washington and Ankara,
each for their own reasons, objected violently to the Cypriot decisions on the
S-300 system. Relying on the potentially destabilizing effects of the system in
the region and its negative impact on any progress on the resolution of the
Cyprus Question, Washington sought the help of influential EU members to
stop the acquisition and deployment of this defensive weapons system. These
combined pressures brought the desired result. The S-300 anti-aircraft missile
system was sent to Greece for storage. Cyprus could not afford to jeopardize
its EU candidacy with either an incident with Turkey or a failure in the talks
that could be attributed to the S-300 decision.

Turkey and the Turkish Cypriot leadership sought to stop the application of Cyprus for EU accession. They relied on a combination of political and
legal arguments to achieve their goal. On the political front, Turkey and the
Turkish Cypriots at first demanded that in order to have progress in the UN-
sponsored talks Cyprus should withdraw its case for EU accession. When it

became apparent that this tactic would not work, they switched to the argument that only a united Cyprus could enter the EU, and only if Turkey was admitted at the same time. For the latter argument Turkey relied on its own legal interpretation of the 1959 independence agreements, arguing that Cyprus could not be a member of any international organization that did not include Turkey. International practice since 1960 proved the fallacy of that argument.

The Luxembourg European Council decision of 12–13 December 1997 did not fulfill Turkey's membership expectations. The council, however, recognized the benefits of accession for both Cypriot communities and for helping to bring about "civil peace and reconciliation." The council urged the government of Cyprus to include representatives of the Turkish Cypriot community in the accession negotiating delegation. On 12 March 1998 President Glafkos Clerides invited the Turkish Cypriot leadership to nominate representatives to be included as full members of the Cypriot team negotiating the accession of Cyprus to the EU. This was an important confidence-building measure on the part of the government of Cyprus. The Turkish Cypriot leadership rejected the offer, arguing that the EU ought to provide for separate negotiations with the illegal regime of the occupied areas. This was a clear Turkish Cypriot attempt to undermine the EU's nonrecognition policy on the Turkish Cypriot pseudo-state. It also indicated the willingness of the occupation regime to subordinate Turkish Cypriot interests to Turkey's political objectives. The EU welcomed the Cypriot initiative and held fast to its position that Cyprus spoke with one voice and that was the voice of the legitimate government of the Republic of Cyprus.

The war of nerves by both Washington and Ankara intensified as the EU decided that Cyprus would become an EU member with or without a solution to the political question. Ankara argued that the accession of Cyprus to the EU would amount to the union of Cyprus to Greece, which was already an EU member. This rather weak argument was based on the emerging European integration. Even though unfounded, this argument was used as a rationalization for the threat of the incorporation of the occupied areas of Cyprus to Turkey. Clear EU warnings to Ankara as to the fallacy of the argument and that the incorporation of the territory of an EU prospective member to Turkey would seal the fate of the Turkish application had the desired result. The Turkish threat never materialized.

Washington in turn warned of the risk of conflict in Cyprus and/or in the Aegean Sea if Cyprus was admitted to the EU and Turkey was not. This threat did not materialize either. Any attempt by Turkey to use force in the region would have ended any prospect for its EU accession. It was an empty threat that proved counterproductive. Anyone familiar with Washington's concern over the deteriorating conditions in the Middle East knew that the United States would not allow a new source of instability in an already unstable region. Both situations turned out to be empty threats and scare tactics that did not change EU policy on Cyprus.

Challenges and Lessons

The preceding sections addressed many of the issues and obstacles involved in the application for EU accession by a small, divided European country. This section will identify some additional issues arising from the Cypriot application case.

As in all accession negotiations, there were organizational and policy coordination problems. The technocratic teams that handled the negotiations with the commission and the diplomatic teams that promoted the Cypriot case in the EU and in the United States had to address all these issues.[11] In charge of the accession negotiations was the former president of the Republic of Cyprus, George Vassiliou. He addressed early on the policy coordination issues among the various government agencies involved in the negotiations. He had the authority to cut through bureaucratic obstacles. His authority derived from the terms of his appointment, the broad political consensus on the importance of accession, and the priority given to accession by the governments of Presidents Clerides and Papadopoulos. The other technical challenge was finding adequate numbers of Cypriot specialists in various facets of domestic and European law. These specialists had to prepare the Cypriot response to all chapters of the accession negotiations. Despite the high percentage of Cypriots with advanced degrees and professional training, Cyprus is a small island with a small population base. The success of the technocratic teams and the policy coordination under the leadership of Vassiliou should be a case study for all future EU applicant states.

The challenge facing the Cypriot diplomats in Washington and in major European capitals at first involved overcoming the lack of interest in the Mediterranean expansion of the EU. Later on, the diplomatic challenge included the promotion of the benefits of accession for the resolution of the Cyprus Question, and overcoming pressures for a resolution prior to the accession of Cyprus to the EU. The latter issue dominated the diplomatic background from the time Cyprus applied for membership until 1 May 2004.

It was stated earlier in this chapter that Cyprus could count on the help of Greece in the accession process. This was true up to a point because the reputation of Greece within the EU was not the best. During the troubled 1990s, Greece had been embroiled in the dispute over the denomination of the Former Yugoslav Republic of Macedonia (FYROM), a dispute that arose following the break-up of Yugoslavia. In addition, there were the ongoing Greek-Turkish problems. These problems dated back to 1973, when Turkey unilaterally attempted to alter the status quo in the Aegean Sea and in 1974 invaded Cyprus. The 1990s were marked by a continuing deterioration in Greek-Turkish relations, which reached a crisis point with the 1996 Imia crisis and the arrest in March 1998 of Kurdish leader Abdullah Ocalan.[12] Thus, in the 1990s Greece was seen by many in the EU as being "part of the problem and not part of the solution" on issues of concern to the EU.

This trend was reversed in the late 90s. Two events contributed to the more positive EU attitude on Greece. The first was the streamlining of the Greek economy and public administration undertaken by the German-trained technocrat Costas Simitis, who became prime minister in 1996. The results of his work began bearing fruit by 1998 when Greece joined the EMU (European Monetary Union). The second was his appointment of George Papandreou as foreign minister in the aftermath of the Öcalan affair. Simitis and Papandreou became the architects of the Greek-Turkish détente, which was expected to have a positive effect not only on Greek-Turkish differences but on the Cyprus Question as well. The challenge for Cypriot diplomacy therefore was how to benefit from the experience and influence of Greece within the EU, without compromising the integrity and independence of the Cypriot application. The Cypriot application had to be promoted on its own merits without creating the impression that it would become one more problem on the EU agenda brought in by Greece.

Looking back at the work of Cypriot diplomacy in support of the EU accession case, one more question needs to be answered. Were there promises made by high-level Cypriot officials prior to the accession of Cyprus to the EU that were not kept by the government of Cyprus? This is an important question because of allegations made by American and certain EU officials following the failed referendum of 24 April 2004 on the Annan plan. Both Presidents Clerides (1993–2003) and Papadopoulos (2003–present) clearly deny this scenario. Cypriot presidents consistently cooperated in the good offices mission of the secretary-general. They accepted the first three plans presented by Kofi Annan (2002–2003) as a basis for negotiations, despite the many concessions they entailed and the fact that Turkey and the Turkish Cypriots never reciprocated in the "give and take" required in any sincere negotiation. Instead, Turkey and the Turkish Cypriots rejected the first three versions of the Annan plan. No Cypriot president could falsely promise to sign and endorse any document prepared by a third party in order to achieve his country's accession to the EU. Moreover, even if such a promise had been made, the secretary-general required that his comprehensive plan would be presented to separate and simultaneous referenda. Nobody could guarantee a positive outcome in the Greek Cypriot referendum, even with the endorsement of the president. Regardless of the influence of political parties in Cyprus, the Greek Cypriot public is known for its independent thinking. This is how 76 percent of the Greek Cypriot voters rejected Annan-V. These voters came from across the political spectrum despite the fact that key political leaders were either in favor of the plan or ambivalent about it. A week before President Papadopoulos's speech to the nation early in April 2004 in which he urged a "no" vote in the referendum, public opinion polls already indicated at least a 70 percent negative vote among the Greek Cypriots. No seasoned Cypriot politician could make promises he could not keep. The allegations made by former EU commissioner for expansion Gunther Verheugen and British foreign secretary Jack Straw in the aftermath of the referendum that EU officials were "tricked" by President Papadopoulos were made in anger because of the outcome of the referendum. These allegations showed that the critics of the Cypriots did not understand Greek Cypriot culture, society, or political behavior. Promising negotiations in good faith to achieve a solution and accepting any solution presented by the secretary-general are two very different things.

One more indication of the Greek Cypriot negotiating goodwill was the invitation extended on 12 March 1998 to the Turkish Cypriot leadership to join the Cypriot EU negotiating team. The Turkish Cypriots were invited as full-fledged members of the negotiating team. They were not required to join as members of the Cypriot government. Not many countries would have taken such a risk in an attempt to create goodwill between the two communities and encourage the Turkish Cypriots to share in the benefits involved in EU accession. Turkey subordinated the economic and social benefits the Turkish Cypriots would derive from the membership of Cyprus in the EU to the futile search to upgrade the political status of the unrecognized regime it set up in the occupied areas. Even at the time of this writing, Turkey insists that the Turkish Cypriot "authorities" negotiate separately with the EU. The aid package agreed upon on 7 July 2004 between the government of the Republic of Cyprus and the EU Commission on behalf of the Turkish Cypriots has not been implemented and has not brought any benefits to the Turkish Cypriots. The Turkish Cypriot aid package included 259 million euros for the period 2004–06, along with trade provisions for the export of products from the occupied areas of Cyprus to the EU and for the movement in both directions across the cease-fire line of goods and services. These measures were intended to contribute to the economic development of the Turkish Cypriot community and to overcome the allegations of the "economic isolation" of the Turkish Cypriots. This point has already been examined.

By the end of 2005, some 120 million euros of the EU Turkish Cypriot aid package had been returned to the community budget because of disagreements over the Turkish Cypriot trade. The Turkish Cypriot leadership and Turkey, with British and U.S. support, sought to link the EU trade and aid provisions with the opening of the ports and the airports in the occupied areas. They also attempted to authorize the proposed trade provisions under article 133 of the EU treaty which covers trade with third countries. The application of article 133 would have met the scenario outlined earlier in this volume about the de facto recognition of the occupied areas by treating that area as an "autonomous area within the EU." The COREPER decision of 24 February 2006 makes it clear that this article does not apply, given that under Protocol 10 of the Cypriot accession to the EU it is the Republic of Cyprus as created in 1960 that acceded to the EU. The application of the *acquis* in the occupied areas has been suspended until the resolution of the political question. This suspension can be revoked only with a unanimous decision of the European Council, a member of which is the Republic of Cyprus.

The Cypriot accession to the EU presents two other challenges. Neither is confined to Cyprus and both require joint actions by the government of the Republic of Cyprus and community institutions. The first involves an understanding by both the Cypriot public and the various officials of the benefits, but also the obligations and responsibilities, entailed in EU membership. Belonging to a complex association undergoing political and economic integration has serious effects on sovereignty, identity, and policy areas which in the past had been in the domestic domain. Many of these issues are now addressed by joint actions and coalition-building at the European Parliament and other community institutions. Integration requires a serious dialogue between

EU institutions and the publics of member states. Public frustration with Brussels showed clearly in the results of the French and Dutch referenda on the European Constitution. In the case of Cyprus, the gap between public understanding of EU institutions and procedures had been widened by the emphasis given early on to the political benefits of accession on the resolution of the Cyprus Question. Now, people and policy-makers are becoming increasingly aware of the complexity of coalition building and the "horse trading" needed to address collectively issues ranging from unemployment to the environment and so on, that is, issues going well beyond the resolution of the Cyprus Question.

The other challenge facing Cyprus and all other members of the EU involves the continuing adjustment to EU law and the implementation of policies and commitments undertaken with the accession agreements and subsequent treaty obligations. This is a continuing process that cannot be set aside once the goal of accession has been achieved. Successful adaptation is the ultimate test of accession for any EU member that aspires to be an effective contributor to European integration.

Turkish Cypriot Responses to the Accession of Cyprus to the EU

This chapter has already outlined the pre-accession responses by Turkey and the Turkish Cypriot leaders to the application of the Republic of Cyprus for membership in the EU. Turkey and the Turkish Cypriots failed to prevent the accession of Cyprus to the EU and to link the accession to the solution of the Cyprus Question and Turkey's European aspirations. By declining to accept the invitation of the government of Cyprus to join the Cypriot EU negotiating team, Turkish Cypriots became mere spectators in the emerging EU of twenty-five nations. These developments, along with encouragement by outside forces: (1) brought about the January–February 2003 Turkish Cypriot demonstrations that led to the replacement of Turkish Cypriot leader Rauf Denktash by Mehmet Ali Talat; (2) contributed to the partial lifting of restrictions on the movement of persons and goods across the cease-fire line that had been imposed by the occupation forces since 1974; and (3) influenced the outcome of the vote by the Turkish Cypriots and Turkish settlers in the referendum on Annan-V.

The Turkish Cypriot response since the accession of the Republic of Cyprus to the EU has involved: (1) a mix of political rationalizations; (2) the repetition of old Turkish Cypriot political positions on the Cyprus Question; (3) reliance on historical inaccuracies; and (4) new attempts to upgrade the status of the regime of the occupied areas.[13] The new Turkish Cypriot leader, Mehmet Ali Talat, continues to challenge the legality of the government of the Republic of Cyprus and, thus, the validity of its signature of the EU Accession Treaty in 2003. Talat's denial overlooks the fact that the EU, like the rest of the international community with the exception of Turkey, recognizes the Republic of Cyprus that was created in 1960 as the sole subject of international law. Talat continues to maintain the fiction that the "Greek Cypriot administration" is not the exclusive governing authority on the island. Borrowing a page from Turkey's policies, Talat defends Turkey's unwillingness to recognize the Republic of Cyprus as required by the EU and opposes the EU policy of linking progress on the resolution of the Cyprus Question with Turkey's EU application. The Turkish Cypriot leader appears to be oblivious to the conditions attached by the EU to the decision to open accession negotiations with Turkey. Instead, Talat accuses the EU of: (1) partiality toward the Greek Cypriots; (2) failing to understand the changes that have taken place in Turkey with the election of Erdogan; (3) failing to appreciate the rise of a new leadership in the Turkish Cypriot community; (4) failing to appreciate the implications of the Turkish Cypriot approval of Annan-V in the 2004 referendum; and (5) failing to link the solution of the Cyprus Question to the accession of Cyprus to the EU. In a memory lapse, Talat also accuses the EU of accepting in its ranks a divided country for the first time in history. It appears that the case of Germany was off Talat's radar scope.

Having accused the EU of all these failures, Talat demands that the EU meet its promise to "end the isolation" of the Turkish Cypriots through direct trade and aid and through the formal opening of ports and airports under Turkish Cypriot control. The clear objective of this demand is the de facto recognition of the occupied areas and implicit acceptance by the EU of Turkey's position that there are two states on the island. These positions show how far removed the Turkish Cypriots and Turkey are from the realities of the Cyprus Question and EU policy. Turkish Cypriots believe that, eventually, the EU will tire of the Cyprus deadlock and come around and accept the Turkish Cypriot positions in order to close the book on Cyprus. In view of what we have discussed in this volume, this is not likely to happen.

This volume has already discussed the European solution to the Cyprus Question. Such a solution will benefit all Cypriots because it will be compatible with the standards of European law and the European Convention. This idea will succeed if those who influence the resolution process take advantage of the opportunities for a just and viable settlement offered by Cyprus's accession to the EU. Unfortunately, countries like the United States and Great Britain continue to rely on the failed policies that have been analyzed in this volume and this chapter.

CHAPTER SIX

Looking Back

THE OPENING CHAPTER of this book examined the forces shaping the political culture and political evolution of postindependence Cyprus. This chapter will focus on: (1) the creation of the Republic of Cyprus and the challenges facing its constitutional evolution; (2) the causes for the breakdown of the political system imposed on Cyprus as a condition of its independence; (3) the attempts to resolve the problems that arose in the implementation of the independence agreements; (4) Turkey's threats to the independence, territorial integrity, and sovereignty of the Republic of Cyprus that culminated in the 1974 Turkish invasion; (5) the political, humanitarian, legal, and economic consequences of the Turkish invasion; and (6) how the interests of powers external to Cyprus have influenced the search for a just, viable, and functional solution to the Cyprus Question.

A Brief Historical Background

Cyprus had been part of the Byzantine Empire. King Richard I, the "Lionheart," of England conquered Cyprus in 1191 A.D. Through the Middle Ages and until 1570 Cyprus remained under Frankish and Venetian rule. The introductory chapter explained how the Ottoman conquest of Cyprus (1570–71) opened a new chapter in the long history of the island. The Ottoman Turks handed Cyprus to the British in 1878. Britain had economic and strategic interests in the eastern Mediterranean and the Middle East. It needed to secure the approaches to the Suez Canal and wanted to contain Russia's imperial designs on the Straits and the eastern Mediterranean. In exchange for protecting the "sick man of Europe" from the designs of imperial Russia and collecting on the Ottoman debt, the 1878 Cyprus Convention handed over the possession and administration of Cyprus to Great Britain. However, technically, Cyprus remained part of the Ottoman Empire until the outbreak of World War I in 1914. At that time, Britain formally annexed Cyprus because Ottoman Turkey aligned itself with Germany in the Great War. The 1923 Lausanne Treaty settled all territorial and political issues left over from World War I in the region. Under the treaty, Turkey also relinquished all its rights and interests in Cyprus. In 1925, Cyprus was declared a Crown colony and remained one until 1960, when it was granted independence.

As shown earlier in this book, Britain's economic neglect of Cyprus, the failure to introduce democratic self-government on the island, and the "divide-and-rule" tactics employed by the British in order to blunt Greek Cypriot political aspirations led to the aborted 1931 Greek Cypriot rebellion and the 1955–59 full-scale Greek Cypriot uprising against British rule. Chapter one examined in detail the enosis movement on Cyprus.

The consequences of British colonial policy were far-reaching and tragic. They systematically cultivated communal separation in all aspects of daily life. They manipulated the Turkish Cypriot community, incited and/or tolerated Turkish Cypriot violent outbreaks against the Greek Cypriots during the anticolonial struggle,[1] and encouraged Turkey to revive its claims on Cyprus, despite the provisions of the 1923 Treaty of Lausanne. Since then, the partition of Cyprus has become a key objective of Turkish foreign and security policy. This was nearly achieved by the presentation of the Macmillan Plan on 19 June 1958.[2]

Britain failed to control the Greek Cypriot uprising despite the deployment of thousands of troops and the violence employed against the population. The violations of human rights by the British forces led to major interstate applications against Britain in the organs of the Council of Europe. The threat of partition under the Macmillan Plan, the repeated but inconclusive appeals by Greece to the UN General Assembly on behalf of Cyprus, the growing intercommunal conflict on Cyprus, and the anxiety of the United States about the effects of the Cyprus Question on NATO's effectiveness and cohesion contributed to secret Greco-Turkish talks. This dialogue led to the 1959 Zurich and London Agreements that granted independence to Cyprus.

The Greek Cypriots and the Fear of Partition

Turkey's interest in the partition of Cyprus needs elaboration. During the Greek Cypriot anticolonial struggle, Greece, Turkey, and the United States flirted with the idea of partition as a solution to the Cyprus Question. Partition was seen as a means of improving Greco-Turkish relations by partially satisfying each country's political aims. It would also remove an irritant in the Western alliance that had been exploited by the Soviets and had affected NATO's cohesion and effectiveness. However, partition carried a serious human cost. It would have required ethnic separation and ethnic cleansing because of the demographic mix of the two major Cypriot communities throughout the island.

This fear of partition has been a key determinant of the Greek Cypriot position in all power-sharing negotiations. For instance, on the issue of local government the Greek Cypriots consistently opposed schemes providing for the geographic grouping of villages with a predominant Turkish Cypriot population. After the problems that arose in the implementation of the Zurich and London Agreements late in 1963, the government of Cyprus became increasingly suspicious of Turkish attempts to create Turkish Cypriot enclaves across the island with their own police and administrative structures. As the Republic of Cyprus gained legitimacy among the Greek Cypriot political elite, the fear of partition was enhanced by schemes that would not only effectively partition Cyprus but also terminate or dissolve the Republic of Cyprus. The United States, Britain, Greece, and Turkey discussed many of these plans behind the back of the government of Cyprus. This was the case with the 1964 Acheson Plan and the 1965 and 1971 Greco-Turkish plans on Cyprus which will be discussed later in this chapter.

The Turkish invasion of 1974 and the ethnic cleansing carried out by the Turkish army imposed the ethnic separation that would be part of a future partition of Cyprus. For the first time since the 1570–71 Ottoman conquest of Cyprus, the island consisted of two largely ethnically cleansed areas. The deterioration in Greek-Turkish relations after 1973 changed Turkey's interest in the de jure partition of Cyprus. Formal partition would have extended the contested Greek-Turkish Aegean boundary all the way to the eastern Mediterranean and could have placed Greece near Turkey's soft underbelly. This is why Turkish policy after 1974, and especially after the 1983 proclamation of the so-called "TRNC" in the occupied areas of Cyprus, focused on constitutional schemes advocating the de facto but not the de jure partition of Cyprus. This was reflected in the Turkish position that there are two autonomous states on Cyprus that can unite in a loose confederation. For this reason, Turkey endorsed Annan-V in 2004. The loose confederation proposed under this plan had all the benefits of effective partition. Turkey and the Turkish Cypriots would be in effective control of the Turkish Cypriot "state," as well as of all of Cyprus through their expanded veto powers and intervention rights granted to them by Annan-V. Moreover, Turkey's security interests were protected by the presence of an emasculated and demilitarized Cyprus, which would not be part of the European defense network. Thus, Annan-V provided for the de facto partition of Cyprus without the risks or costs of de jure partition. This was one of the many reasons for the Greek Cypriot rejection of Annan-V.

The 1959 Zurich and London Agreements

Following secret consultations between the governments of Greece and Turkey, the Greek and Turkish prime ministers, Constantine Karamanlis and Adnan Menderes, met in Zurich, Switzerland. On 11 February 1959, the two countries agreed to a blueprint for the independence of Cyprus. The blueprint was largely the work of the Turkish delegation. On 19 February 1959, the same leaders met in London with British prime minister Harold Macmillan and representatives of the two Cypriot communities to confirm their final agreement for the independence of Cyprus. Independence had not been the primary goal of the Greek Cypriot anticolonial movement. It came to be accepted as an alternative to the dreaded partition under the Macmillan Plan. Greece also exerted maximum pressure on Archbishop Makarios and the other Greek Cypriot leaders who were present to accept the agreement. The constitution of the new republic was to be based on the Zurich and London

Agreements. Cyprus became independent on 16 August 1960. England accepted the independence of Cyprus as long as Greece and Turkey agreed on the independence terms and Britain's regional security interests were protected. The agreement relieved Britain of the political, legal, and economic costs of the Greek Cypriot uprising.

Three basic treaties were the foundation of the independent Republic of Cyprus. The first was the Treaty of Establishment. It included the fundamental laws of the new republic. The treaty contained rigid clauses making constitutional amendments of fundamental laws a virtual impossibility in the absence of prior agreement by the three guarantor powers. The treaty also granted Britain to maintain Sovereign Base Areas (SBAs) on ninety-nine square miles, i.e., 2.7 percent, of the territory of the new republic. Since then, the issue of the SBAs and the access rights Britain enjoys all over Cyprus have become an important bilateral issue. This point will be examined below.

Some controversial, complicated, and divisive provisions of the independence agreements included:[3]

- the division along strict ethnic lines. The 82 percent Greek Cypriot community included the small Armenian and Maronite communities.
- the renunciation of union with Greece or the partition of Cyprus.
- extensive vetoes in all major policy areas by the 18 percent Turkish Cypriot minority.
- the president would be a Greek Cypriot. The Greek Cypriots would elect the president. The Turkish Cypriots would elect a Turkish Cypriot vice-president who had veto powers over all fundamental laws passed by the House of Representatives and the decisions of the Council of Ministers.
- the Council of Ministers (Cabinet) consisted of ten members, three of whom would be Turkish Cypriots appointed by the vice-president. One of the major ministries (foreign affairs, defense, finance) would be entrusted to a Turkish Cypriot.
- a 70:30 ratio applied to the Civil Service.
- a 60:40 ratio applied to the police and the Cypriot army.
- members of the House of Representatives would be elected by separate rolls in each community. The House could not amend the fundamental aspects of the constitution. Separate majorities were required on laws affecting municipalities, taxes, or modifications to the electoral law. Fifteen of the fifty seats in the House were reserved for Turkish Cypriots. Because of the separate voting majorities in the House of Representatives, a minority among the Turkish Cypriots could thwart the will of the majority. This became a major cause for the breakdown of the 1959 agreements late in 1963.
- the Supreme Constitutional Court and the High Court of Justice were presided over by neutral foreign judges, who held the balance of power on all split decisions. Offences committed by members of one ethnic community were to be tried by judges from that community. Cases involving Greek and Turkish Cypriots would be heard by mixed courts.

- separate Communal Chambers were set up to address religious, educational, cultural, and charitable issues for each community. In addition, these chambers regulated questions of personal status, cooperative and credit societies, and related communal issues.
- separate municipalities were envisaged for the five largest cities of Cyprus, despite the fact that in most cases the population and properties were intermixed.

This was not only a costly but also a divisive constitutional provision.

The other two major treaties associated with the independence of Cyprus were the Treaties of Guarantee and Alliance. Under the former, Greece, Turkey, and Britain were given the right to intervene collectively or individually, if collective action was not possible, in the affairs of the republic to re-establish the status quo created by the independence treaties. The treaty was silent on the issue of military intervention. Otherwise, it would have been in conflict with the provisions of the UN Charter. Turkey, however, interpreted the silence of the treaty to include military action. It was under such a unilateral interpretation that Turkey invaded Cyprus in 1974.

The Treaty of Alliance in turn called for military cooperation between Greece and Turkey and the emerging small Cypriot military force to protect Cyprus. The treaty provided for the stationing of a Greek military contingent of 950 men and a Turkish contingent of 650 men on the island. For the first time since the British takeover of Cyprus in 1878, Turkish troops legally returned to Cyprus. Members of the Turkish contingent became the conduit of military assistance to the Turkish Cypriots during the 1963–74 Turkish Cypriot rebellion. The Turkish contingent also played a critical role during Turkey's 1974 invasion of Cyprus. Moreover, various other annexes and appendices were attached to the independence treaties enhancing the political role of the guarantor powers and limiting the independence of the new republic.

The 1959 Independence Agreements: An Assessment

Even though the 1959 agreements gave Cyprus independence, it was a controlled independence. The minority vetoes, Britain's access rights in and around Cyprus, the Treaty of Guarantee and its foreign intervention provisions, and the stationing of foreign troops on Cypriot soil were proof of this. Thus, the burden that fell on the government of the Republic of Cyprus was how to secure the independence, sovereignty, and territorial integrity of the republic and assure the place of Cyprus as an equal member of the international community. The constitutional provisions summarized earlier were the clear outcome of the British divide-and-rule policy and of the consequences of Britain's incitement of Turkey's involvement in Cyprus in order to blunt Greek Cypriot political demands. Thus, in 1959, as in the current situation in Cyprus, the Cyprus Question was not addressed in its real dimensions. It was always seen through the prism of great power relations and their strategic interests. This distorted the true dimensions of the question.

As problems arose in the implementation of these agreements, the Greek Cypriots came to see the agreements as unjust and imposed. In contrast, the Turkish Cypriots considered the rights granted to them by the agreements and Turkey's guarantor role as the minimum protection of their status as a co-founder community of the Republic of Cyprus rather than as a minority in need of protection. By 1963, the Greek Cypriots, confronted with a constitutional deadlock in the House of Representatives, sought amendments to the constitution. The proposed amendments were intended to bring the constitution in compliance with democratic norms and the rule of law, and to assure the functionality of the political system.

The implementation problems and the frustrations of the Greek Cypriots had been anticipated. The independence agreements were one of the most flagrant cases of unequal and imposed treaties in recent international law. The agreements were negotiated in the absence of both Cypriot communities and were imposed on them under the threat of the partition of Cyprus. The agreements were never presented to the Cypriot House of Representatives for ratification. Moreover, the limitations on the sovereignty of Cyprus, as evidenced by Britain's access rights in and around Cyprus, the intervention provisions of the Treaty of Guarantee, and the attempt to limit the domestic and foreign policy independence of Cyprus,[4] were clear proof that Cyprus had no voice in the independence negotiations. Foreign international law authorities[5] and even a classified analysis by the Bureau of Intelligence and Research of the U.S. Department of State[6] had concluded that these sui generis agreements were unprecedented and likely to create implementation problems. In many respects, the U.S. Department of State analysis proved to be prophetic. The constitutional amendments proposed by President Makarios late in 1963 were intended to overcome the dysfunctionalities and problems that that analysis had identified. The deadlock in the House of Representatives over the proposed municipal partition and the Turkish Cypriot blackmail veto on taxation legislation were clear proof of the dysfunctional constitution. Even UN mediator Galo Plaza in 1965 described the 1960 Cypriot constitution as an "oddity."

Finally, the independence agreements were in direct conflict with fundamental principles of international law and the UN Charter. There was no other country, with the possible exception of some members of the Soviet bloc, where foreign powers could legally intervene and dictate the domestic and foreign policy of an independent and sovereign UN member.

In November 1963, in an attempt to save the Republic of Cyprus from the problems created by the implementation of these divisive and dysfunctional agreements, President Makarios proposed thirteen amendments to the Cypriot constitution for discussion with the Turkish Cypriots. Without discussion and before the Turkish Cypriots had a chance to respond, Turkey rejected outright the proposed amendments. History has yet to clarify the role and motives of the British high commissioner to Nicosia in the drafting and presentation of these amendments. Available documentation indicates that Makarios had discussed the amendments and had gotten the approval of the British high commissioner. Ironically enough, eleven years later, in the summer of 1974, the proposed amendments had been incorporated in the agreement reached between the Greek and Turkish Cypriots in the UN-sponsored intercommunal talks. That agreement was scuttled by the coup against the government of Cyprus carried out by the junta ruling Greece at the time.

As a concluding note, the reader should be reminded of the earlier discussion on the Annan plan and the secretary-general's insistence on holding separate and simultaneous referenda on Annan-V. He and his advisors had learned a lesson from the 1959–60 imposed independence treaties. Kofi Annan wanted his solution to be approved by a referendum so that no one could later challenge the legitimacy of the derogations, of Turkey's expanded intervention rights, and of Britain's new powers over the SBAs that were included in his arbitration plan.

Political and Legislative Challenges 1960–63

In view of the circumstances leading to the creation of the Republic of Cyprus in 1960, the political leadership of Cyprus, Greece, Turkey, and Britain had a special responsibility to make the dysfunctional and divisive system created in Zurich and London work. Unfortunately, this did not prove to be the case. Suspicions ran deep among members of both communities in Cyprus about the motives of the motherlands and about each community's motives in accepting the Zurich and London Agreements.

A first challenge for both Cypriot communities was the creation of a legitimate polity that placed national interests above communal interests and above the interests of the motherlands. It meant outgrowing communal divisions and looking beyond the anticolonial revolutionary experience in order to construct a legitimate national political order based on the rule of law and the equality of all citizens. This was a major challenge for a former colony with no experience in national, let alone bicommunal, politics. In that sense, Cyprus faced a predicament not uncommon to other societies coming out of colonial rule. The problem was compounded by communal cleavages as well as by political cleavages within each community. This was especially true in the Greek Cypriot community, where the church and the conservative political elite viewed with suspicion the influential Communist Party (AKEL) because of its questionable commitment to the anticolonial struggle. It took the great conciliatory skills of President Makarios to come up with a power-sharing formula among the emerging Greek Cypriot political parties in the aftermath of the first free national parliamentary elections. The problem was further compounded by the involvement of the two motherlands in communal politics. While the Greek involvement ended with the 1974 coup, Turkey continues to manipulate and control Turkish Cypriot politics.

Another challenge facing the new republic was the fact that independence had not been the goal of either community. Since 1878, the Greek Cypriot goal had been self-determination and union with Greece. This has already been discussed above in the first chapter. Thus, it took a concerted effort on the part of key Greek Cypriot political leaders to strengthen the legitimacy of their new polity, especially in view of the divisive nature of the constitution and the manner by which it was imposed on the majority community. As the Greek Cypriot political leadership gained experience, maturity, and confidence in the face of external threats and the threat of partition of their state, the legitimacy of the new republic grew in the eyes of the majority community. If there were any doubts, these were overcome by the 1974 coup in Cyprus sponsored by the junta ruling Greece at the time, the 1974 Turkish invasion, the continuing occupation of nearly 37 percent of the territory of the republic, and the experience Cypriot leaders accumulated by working in various international fora. The accession of Cyprus to the EU on 1 May 2004 was the apex of the legitimization of the Republic of Cyprus.

The third challenge facing Cyprus and its government was the protection of the sovereignty, territorial integrity, and independence of the republic. This challenge was the result of the conditions leading to the creation of the Republic of Cyprus and of the consequences of the divisive constitution imposed on the new state. The 1963 constitutional deadlock led to the collapse of the Zurich formula and intercommunal clashes and threats of military intervention by Turkey in 1964 and 1967. The United States was concerned about the impact of the Cyprus Question on NATO's cohesion and effectiveness and about the risk of a Greco-Turkish conflict over Cyprus. It therefore urged the two guarantors to seek ways to defuse the crisis. This included the partition of the island.[7] Washington also promoted formulas that would lead to the dissolution of the Republic of Cyprus,[8] and sought ways to replace the elected president of Cyprus with a leader more amenable to American and Turkish designs.[9]

It is not surprising that the Greek Cypriot leadership devoted its energy to the internationalization of the Cyprus Question in order to protect the sovereignty, territorial integrity, and independence of Cyprus. These events also explain why the Greek Cypriot leadership, both before and after independence, opposed any schemes that implied the territorial division of Cyprus. This is also why Greek Cypriots were opposed to the separate municipalities called for under the independence agreements.[10] This fear of partition has influenced Greek Cypriot attitudes and policies since the mid-50s.

Another issue raised by the independence agreements remains unresolved, that is, the status of the British bases on Cypriot soil. The so-called SBAs are one more manifestation of the unequal treaties that brought Cyprus to independence. The Cypriots had no say in the granting of 2.7 percent of the territory of their island to Great Britain, nor in any of Britain's extensive access rights in and around Cyprus. Both the unilateral access rights and the extent of sovereignty enjoyed by the British bases violate all concepts of national sovereignty under contemporary international law. This infringement of Cypriot sovereignty is evidenced by the activities carried out on the SBAs. The bases include extensive military logistical facilities, a major military airfield, state-of-the-art military medical facilities, and the most sophisticated electronic monitoring installations in the region.[11] These monitoring facilities cover a huge geographic area, from southern Russia to the Middle East and to northeast Africa. Even though Britain is a member of both NATO and the EU, these facilities remain outside the NATO framework and, more recently, outside the EU's common defense policy. They are widely used by the U.S. National Security Agency, while American U-2 spy flights operate regularly out of the Akrotiri airbase. These facilities were of primary significance during the Gulf

War and subsequent Anglo-American invasion of Iraq in March 2003. The activities carried out from these facilities show no regard for EU or Cypriot policy, let alone Cypriot sovereignty. They are one more remnant of Cyprus's colonial past.

The status of the SBAs remains controversial. There are legal questions not only regarding the manner by which they were acquired by Britain, but also about the actual extent of sovereignty enjoyed by Britain on these bases. Many of these issues have yet to be tested in British or other courts. Successive British governments have studiously avoided bringing on appeal cases arising from actions of their own authorities on the SBAs because of uncertainties existing over the status of the SBAs under the independence agreements. Moreover, British governments have failed to reimburse the Republic of Cyprus over $1 billion in leases and fees from their use of Cypriot facilities. Britain argues that these payments will be made following a future settlement of the Cyprus Question so that both communities can benefit from these funds. This is a weak argument, given the presence of legal mechanisms for the distribution of these funds to the Turkish Cypriots. The bases employ local labor, including Turkish Cypriots, who are organized in mainly left-wing unions. This may explain why AKEL, the Communist Party of Cyprus, has been unwilling to mount a full-scale challenge to these "imperialist" facilities. It is only recently that labor issues have become more prominent, as Britain announced privatization plans affecting various functions on the bases. The bases have also become a source of friction over health and environmental issues as a result of the effect of electronic emissions from powerful new electronic antennas.

The issues raised by the SBAs explain Britain's interest to clarify problem areas and expand its rights in the SBAs. The secretary-general's arbitration plan (Annan-V) provided the means to that end. The failure of the plan in the 24 April 2004 referendum continues to keep these issues in limbo.

The love/hate relationship between Cyprus and Britain reflects the Greek Cypriot suspicion of Britain's motives, due to the cumulative effects of its actions in Cyprus throughout the twentieth century. Britain's role in the five plans submitted by Kofi Annan and its postreferendum behavior has not helped Britain's credibility. Even though Britain's policy may effectively promote the de facto partition of Cyprus, it has studiously avoided actions implying the revocation of the 1959 Zurich and London Agreements. Any questioning of these agreements would likely affect the status of the SBAs. This is why Britain attempted to secure its base rights through the referenda called for under the Annan plan. For various political reasons, no Cypriot government has formally challenged the status of the bases. However, in recent years, Greek Cypriot politicians have begun raising questions about the bases and the moneys owed to the Republic of Cyprus by Britain, and have begun linking their toleration of these bases to Britain's behavior on the Cyprus Question. Greek Cypriot think tanks have also discussed this issue in conferences and position papers. For the time, the issue of the bases remains in diplomatic reserve as Cypriot governments appear unwilling to open a new front in the war to secure the independence and sovereignty of their republic.

The 1963 Turkish Cypriot Rebellion and the Response of the United Nations

On the evening of 21 December 1963, a minor incident involving a police patrol and a suspicious car driven by Turkish Cypriots led to major intercommunal violence instigated by Turkish Cypriot extremists. This was the work of the TMT, which, as shown earlier, was organized, trained, and equipped by Turkey's special forces. The outbreak of violence appears to have been based on a prearranged plan.

Turkish Cypriot cabinet members, members of the House of Representatives, and civil servants withdrew from the government. Fazil Kutchuk, the Turkish Cypriot vice-president, declared that the Republic of Cyprus "had ceased to exist" and that the 1960 constitution was "dead."[12] The plan for the partition of Cyprus was set in motion. TMT members, led by Turkish Army officers and assisted by the Turkish contingent stationed in Cyprus under the Treaty of Alliance, deployed in various sections of Nicosia. Arguing that the Turkish Cypriot minority faced annihilation, they began forcibly uprooting the Turkish Cypriots and placing them in enclaves under TMT control. This was the first step toward the geographic separation of the two communities. These plans were included in captured documents dated September 1963 and signed by Kutchuk and Rauf Denktash, the president of the Turkish Cypriot Communal Chamber.

The growing intercommunal violence and Turkish threats of unilateral military intervention led to an emergency conference in London on 15 January 1964 involving the guarantor powers, the government of Cyprus, and the Turkish Cypriots. It became apparent that the purpose of the meeting aimed at the placement of an international force on Cyprus under NATO auspices. An intergovernmental committee consisting of governments supplying contingents would offer political direction to the force. This was a clear attempt to displace and bypass the elected government of Cyprus. The government of Cyprus rejected the proposal. Instead, the matter was brought to the UN Security Council, while British forces stationed on the island carried out peacekeeping duties. The "green line" currently dividing the city of Nicosia was the product of this peacekeeping operation. Recent revelations indicate that British special forces may have been assisting the Turkish Cypriot rebellion.[13]

The weeks preceding the discussion of the Cyprus Question at the Security Council were full of behind-the-scenes diplomatic maneuvering. Washington was in control of these initiatives because it was fearful of a Soviet exploitation of the dispute, if not also its involvement in the dispute. The U.S. government was also concerned about the possibility of a Greco-Turkish conflict because of Cyprus and the reprisals undertaken by the Turkish government against the remaining members of the Greek minority of Istanbul. That community had already been decimated in 1955 by a pogrom carried out under the Menderes government. The latest expulsions virtually eliminated a community that had lived in Istanbul since antiquity and whose rights were protected by the 1923 Treaty of Lausanne. The fate of the Ecumenical Orthodox patriarchate was also at stake.

Washington recognized the need for revisions to the independence agreements. First, however, any revisions would have to be approved by Turkey and Greece. Meanwhile, President Makarios of Cyprus sought the more secure environment of the United Nations to protect his country's sovereignty and bring about revision to the independence agreements. He feared that the proposed NATO involvement would place alliance interests above those of Cyprus. The United States, Great Britain, and Turkey would have controlling influence on the matter in the organization. In contrast, in the United Nations Makarios could count on support from the Soviet Union, the Eastern European bloc, and the nonaligned, among others. The presence of these countries could defuse actions threatening the sovereignty, independence, and territorial integrity of Cyprus.

One needs to remember the international and regional context of this phase of the Cyprus Question. The crisis on Cyprus followed on the heels of the Soviet-American confrontations over Berlin and Cuba. In the eastern Mediterranean and the Middle East, the Soviet Union was making its presence and interests felt through military advisors and military assistance programs to Arab countries. The Soviets also established a naval presence that culminated in the formation of the Fifth Eskadra that shadowed the U.S. Sixth Fleet in the Mediterranean through the end of the Cold War. The political instability in the eastern Mediterranean and the Middle East was also evident in the two major wars between the Arabs and the Israelis in 1967 and 1973 which risked a Soviet-American confrontation.

The Soviet warning of 7 February 1964 to the United States, Britain, Turkey, and others not to intervene in Cyprus heightened these American fears. It was in this context that U.S. general Lyman L. Lemnitzer, commander of NATO, visited Greece and Turkey on 28 January 1964. He was successful in averting a unilateral Turkish military intervention in Cyprus and set the stage for NATO's attempted involvement there. The Lemnitzer mission was followed by the 12 February 1964 visit to Nicosia of U.S. presidential envoy George W. Ball. His mission aimed to gain the consent of the government of Cyprus for the proposed NATO plan and, failing that, to seek alternative Greek Cypriot leaders willing to do that. He failed in both objectives, even though he had the backing of the guarantor powers, including Greece. At the time, Greece was in the midst of a political crisis that culminated in the 21 April 1967 NATO-sanctioned military coup. For both ideological and practical reasons, Greece could not defy Washington's wishes, despite the opposition of Greek public opinion.

As a result of these maneuverings, the government of Cyprus brought its case to the UN Security Council despite Anglo-American objections. After a series of meetings, the Security Council adopted unanimously two very important resolutions whose effect has since influenced the course of the Cyprus Question. The first was Resolution 186 of 4 March 1964 and the second Resolution 187 of 13 March 1964. These resolutions (1) established the UN secretary-general's mission of good offices aiming at a peaceful solution on the basis of an agreed settlement in accordance with the UN Charter; (2) created the UN peacekeeping force on Cyprus (UNFICYP); (3) reaffirmed the sovereignty, territorial integrity, and continuing existence of the Republic of Cyprus; and (4) reaffirmed the continuity and legitimacy of the government of Cyprus, despite the walkout of its Turkish Cypriot members.

Both resolutions were a major success of Cypriot diplomacy. Effective March 1964, the United Nations formally engaged in both a peacekeeping and a peacemaking process lasting to this day. Earlier chapters have examined the reasons for the failure of UN peacemaking initiatives. The importance of the affirmation of the legitimacy of the Cypriot government and the continuity of the Republic of Cyprus cannot be overstated. It became the mainstay of Cypriot diplomatic efforts countering schemes that would dissolve the Republic of Cyprus and lead to a Greco-Turkish partition of the island. These threats started in the spring of 1964 and culminated in the Annan initiatives of 2004. The United States and Britain, the prime movers behind these schemes, ended up supporting both resolutions. They had no other options, especially as the risk of regional conflict increased. As for the president of Cyprus, the Security Council's involvement in the supervision of both the UN peacekeeping and UN peacemaking activities was an assurance that Cyprus could avoid NATO- and U.S.-inspired negative scenaria intended to serve the alliance's and Turkey's strategic needs rather than those of Cyprus.

The Troubled Peacemaking Process

The limited UN presence and jurisdiction on Cyprus curbed the level of intercommunal violence but did not fully eliminate it. Meanwhile, TMT-controlled Turkish Cypriot enclaves sprang up across the island. Turkey continued its threats of unilateral intervention against Cyprus. A sharply worded ultimatum by U.S. president Lyndon B. Johnson on 5 June 1964 stopped an impending Turkish invasion. This ultimatum became the rationalization as well as the catalyst for Turkey's progressive adoption of a more independent foreign policy during the Cold War. This tactic became a means of pressuring Washington, which was accused of abandoning its ally. It should be noted that the Johnson ultimatum did not imply an American disagreement with Turkey's objectives on Cyprus. Rather, it was the result of Turkish tactics that risked the possibility of a Soviet-American confrontation over Cyprus.

Despite UN involvement, independent U.S. initiatives on Cyprus continued. President Johnson invited Greek prime minister George Papandreou and Turkish prime minister Ismet Inonu to separate meetings in Washington on 22 and 24 June 1964, respectively. The purpose was to "sell" to the two countries ideas for a Greco-Turkish resolution of the Cyprus Question behind the back of the government of Cyprus. These initiatives culminated in variations of a plan that came to be known as the Acheson Plan on Cyprus.[14] The presentation was preceded on 2 July 1964 by American warnings to Greece that the United States would not intervene again to halt either a Turkish invasion or a Greco-Turkish conflict. Acheson presented his first version of the plan on 4 July 1964. The Cypriots had not been invited, even though the plan would determine the fate of their state. The plan essentially called for the dissolution of the Republic of Cyprus and its union with Greece. Under a secret protocol that would not be presented to the Greek Parliament for ratification, Greece, in the interest of NATO security policy, would grant Turkey a military base on the northeast section of Cyprus amounting to 14-18 percent of the republic's territory. To make the plan more acceptable to Greece, a later version of the plan called for a fifty-year lease to Turkey of the proposed base area. Even though the revised version of the plan was initially acceptable to Greece, under pressure from Cyprus the Greek government rejected Acheson's proposals. Turkey also rejected the plan, because the fifty-year lease provision did not satisfy its partitionist objectives. In addition to the concessions on Cyprus, Greece was to make minor territorial concessions on its northeast frontier with Turkey and turn over to Turkey the Dodecanese island of Kastelorizo.

The period starting in the fall of 1963 and culminating in the Greek-sponsored coup against the government of Cyprus on 15 July 1974 was one of tension between Athens and Nicosia. This was a period of political instability in Greece during which the governments in power, for both ideological and political survival reasons, depended on American support and were susceptible to American pressure. Athens continued to view itself as the "national center of Hellenism" and was annoyed by Nicosia's independent policies. Moreover, these policies were supported by the nonaligned and Eastern blocs. Athens was also concerned that the problems on Cyprus would seal the fate of the Greek minority in Istanbul and lead to a Greco-Turkish confrontation. Finally, like Washington, Athens was fearful of the presence of a large and disciplined Communist Party on the island. No Communist organizations were allowed to operate in Greece at that time. Greece did not favor the presentation by President Makarios of the proposed constitutional amendments. The Cyprus issue had strong public support in Greece, and successive Cypriot governments capitalized on it to influence Greek policy. The final Greek rejection of the Acheson Plan was an example of this influence. All this was lost when the junta seized power in Greece on 21 April 1967. Thus, in contrast to the relations between the Turkish Cypriots and Ankara, the relations between Nicosia and Athens were often strained as their foreign policy goals frequently diverged. Following the 1974 restoration of democracy in Greece, relations between the two countries have been strengthened as Athens accepted Nicosia as an equal.

The Subversion of Peacemaking

The good offices of the secretary-general commenced in March 1964. This, however, did not stop behind-the-scenes U.S.-sponsored diplomatic initiatives or Turkey's threats against the Republic of Cyprus. On 7 and 8 August 1964, the Turkish Air Force carried out bombing raids across Cyprus, causing serious casualties. It took another Soviet warning and another Security Council resolution (No. 193/1964) to stop the deteriorating conditions on Cyprus.

The disregard of the UN peacemaking was manifested in at least three other ways between 1965 and 1967. The first was the rejection by the United States and Turkey of the report by UN mediator on Cyprus Galo Plaza. His report of 26 March 1965 remains one of the most significant documents ever to be written on the Cyprus Question and its resolution.[15] The report questioned the federalism demanded by Turkey for both functional and humanitarian reasons, was critical of the disproportionate minority vetoes that were part of the constitution of 1960, and advocated the protection of minority rights under the European Convention and the organs available under the convention.

The second was the continuation of secret diplomacy in the search of a final solution to the Cyprus Question through a Greco-Turkish agreement. This took two forms:

- The meeting in Paris on 17 December 1965 between Greek foreign minister Admiral John Toumbas and his Turkish counterpart, Ihsan Sabri Caglayangil, following a series of Greco-Turkish secret talks on Cyprus. They initialed a protocol providing for the union of Cyprus to Greece with various concessions to Turkey, including the cession to Turkey of Dhekelia, one of the British SBAs. This offer had Britain's consent. It was intended to overcome Turkey's objections to the Acheson Plan. This protocol was never implemented since the Greek government lost a parliamentary vote of confidence on issues unrelated to Cyprus.
- The meetings in Kesan, Turkey, and Alexandroupolis, Greece, between Greek and Turkish prime ministers Konstantinos Kollias and Suleiman Demirel on 9–10 September 1967. Capitalizing on the weak diplomatic position of the junta that seized control of the Greek government a few months earlier, Turkey rejected outright the Greek proposals, which were found to be based on the failed ideas of the Acheson Plan.

Soon after the 1967 Arab-Israeli War, Turkey once more threatened to invade Cyprus. It took the urgent dispatch of U.S. emissary Cyrus Vance and U.S. warnings to all involved to stop the threatened November 1967 Turkish invasion.[16] This was one more indication of the limited UN peacemaking mandate that became even more pronounced when Turkey actually invaded Cyprus on 20 July 1974.

Despite these developments, the government of Cyprus, in cooperation with the good offices of the secretary-general, took various measures to restore normalcy on the island which reduced intercommunal violence and tensions. Economic incentives were offered to Turkish Cypriots willing to abandon the TMT-operated enclaves and return to the safety of their homes. In the aftermath of the November crisis, the Greek and Turkish Cypriot communities commenced a dialogue under the good offices of the secretary-general. Following informal contacts, the discussions commenced on 24 June 1968. Constitutional experts from Greece and Turkey joined the talks early in 1972.[17] Their aim was to prepare an amended constitution for Cyprus. That effort came to a successful conclusion some thirty-six hours before the coup staged in Nicosia on 15 July 1974 by the junta ruling Greece at the time, along with extremist Greek Cypriot opponents of President Makarios.[18] The coup provided the pretext for Turkey's invasion of Cyprus on 20 July 1974.

The ironic conclusion of the 1968–74 round of UN-sponsored intercommunal talks was that Rauf Denktash, acting on behalf of the Turkish

Cypriot community, had accepted virtually all the revisions to the Cypriot constitution that President Makarios had proposed in 1963. What is even more remarkable was that these talks succeeded despite the continued secret Greco-Turkish contacts on a Cyprus solution and systematic attempts by the Greek junta to subvert the government of Cyprus. These actions included:

- The controversial Greco-Turkish "consensus" that was reached in Lisbon on 3–4 June 1971 between Greek deputy foreign minister Christos Xanthopoulos-Palamas and Turkish foreign minister Osman Olcay. The meeting took place on the sidelines of the NATO foreign ministers meeting. The "consensus" consisted of a Greco-Turkish commitment to a final solution to the Cyprus Question based on the partition of Cyprus if the ongoing intercommunal talks failed.
- Ultimata addressed by the government of Greece to President Makarios to bring his policy in the intercommunal talks in conformity with Greek and Turkish positions.[19] Failure to comply would result in "bitter consequences" for Cyprus.
- The organization and arming by the Greek junta of EOKA-B. This was a Cypriot extremist organization seeking to undermine the elected government of Cyprus and assassinate President Makarios. This was a different organization from the one that led the struggle against the British in 1955–59.
- The Greek junta's ultimatum that President Makarios turn over to UNFICYP weapons his government had ordered from Czechoslovakia in January 1972.
- The American rejection of the 1971 proposal by UN secretary-general U Thant for a mediation initiative by nonpermanent members of the UN Security Council under the chairmanship of France. This was one more indication that the United States was likely to oppose any UN initiatives that were not in accordance with American and Turkish views.

The Coup and the 1974 Turkish Invasion

On 15 July 1974, the junta ruling Greece at the time, in cooperation with Greek Cypriot extremist elements, carried out a coup against the democratically elected government of Cyprus. Using this criminal act as a pretext, Turkey invaded Cyprus five days later. In a two-stage invasion and despite cease-fire calls by the UN Security Council, within a month Turkey occupied 36.2 percent of the territory of the Republic of Cyprus. Turkey justified its action under the terms of the Treaty of Guarantee, even though military action was not included in the terms of the treaty. Turkey claimed that it acted to protect the Turkish Cypriots and restore the status quo ante in Cyprus. Both claims are false. No Turkish Cypriots were harmed during the coup. It was a purely internal Greek Cypriot affair. Nor has anyone proven that the aim of the coup was to unite Cyprus with Greece. As for the Turkish claim of acting to restore the status quo ante in Cyprus, history has shown otherwise. Turkey's aim was and remains the de facto partition of Cyprus. The 1983 unilateral declaration of independence by the "TRNC," the pseudo-state set up in the occupied areas by the Turkish Army, is clear proof.

The events of 15 July to 15 August 1974 require further analysis. The crisis on Cyprus occurred as Washington was going through the final stages of the Watergate crisis and the resignation of President Nixon. U.S. secretary of state Henry Kissinger single handedly defined and executed American foreign policy. Until then, the United States and/or the Soviet Union had stepped in to stop a unilateral Turkish invasion. Even though Washington had warned Greece and Cyprus in its 1964 ultimatum to Prime Minister Inonu that it would not again intervene in another crisis with Turkey, it did so in November 1967. Why did the United States and the Soviets act differently in 1974?

President Makarios had escaped earlier assassination attempts. He also escaped when the coupists attacked the Presidential Palace in Nicosia on 15 July 1974. Even though Makarios, the symbol of Cypriot independence and sovereignty, was alive, his political freedom had been considerably curtailed. He was in temporary exile in London and 36.2 percent of his country was under Turkish occupation. The American involvement in the Nicosia coup is still being debated. The CIA had been actively involved both with the Greek junta and in funding anti-Makarios extremist groups. The situation had many parallels to the U.S. role in Chile and the coup against the Allende government. At a minimum, the U.S. involvement was a sin of omission. The U.S. government knew about the coup and chose not to do anything about it. There is good evidence, however, to suggest that the coup may have been a sin of commission. In that case, the collapsing junta in Athens and the Nixon presidency in Washington created unusual conditions for intervention in Cyprus and for crisis management.

Kissinger's first concern was to stabilize the situation in Athens and to prevent a Greco-Turkish conflict. He was successful in both objectives. The crisis in Cyprus gave Kissinger the opportunity to engineer a solution to the question that had defied him and his predecessors until then. Such a solution would finally satisfy American and Turkish security needs. In pure nineteenth-century style, the student of Metternich's diplomacy stood ready to manipulate the balance of power in Cyprus to achieve the desired end. Working in his favor was the newly attained Soviet-American détente and the understanding that Cyprus fell into a gray area of primary interest to the United States. In an interview soon after the second Turkish invasion, Kissinger was complimentary to the Soviets. He suggested that the Soviet role should be judged by what the USSR "did not do" rather than what the Soviets did in the case of Cyprus. This was a clear reference to Soviet behavior in earlier crises.

The Soviet inaction in 1974 has to be seen in various contexts. This included the emerging Soviet-American détente and the tacit acceptance that each superpower had a vital sphere of interests. The Soviets were not ready to undermine détente over an incident in a gray zone of primary American interest. Moreover, despite rhetorical exercises and occasional threats as in 1964, Soviet policy had not effectively promoted new ideas for a solution to the Cyprus Question. The Soviet proposals for an international conference on Cyprus and the demilitarization of Cyprus played well in the press and in the United Nations. However, there was no serious follow-up on these proposals.

Moreover, an internationally isolated junta carried out the Nicosia coup. They installed a right-wing dictator in Cyprus who lasted only a few days. The Soviets did not feel obligated to rescue such regimes and risk the advantages of détente or the informally expanded access rights the Soviets enjoyed in the Turkish Straits.[20] The victim of all these calculations was Cyprus.

Despite urgent consultations in Ankara, Athens, and London, Kissinger's policy was clear. He did nothing to prevent the coup in Nicosia or to warn the recognized government of Cyprus about the impending coup. Although Washington had the ability to intervene and stop the Turkish invasion, it did not do so.[21] On the contrary, it is alleged that Washington discouraged a proposed British deployment in and around Cyprus and that the Sixth Fleet intercepted a Greek convoy dispatched to Cyprus by the democratic government that took over in Greece following the collapse of the Greek junta. Kissinger described Turkey's invasion as a "small scale" military action and took no practical measures to avert the collapse of the hastily called Geneva talks among the guarantor powers and the government of Cyprus following the first Turkish invasion. The choreographed collapse of the Geneva talks led to the second invasion of Cyprus by Turkey on 14 August 1974. Turkey had the upper hand throughout the summer 1974 crisis on Cyprus. It had the distinct military advantage and Kissinger's support, and it could count on American support for refusing the early and complete withdrawal of its troops from Cyprus despite calls by the UN General Assembly (Resolution 3212, 1 November 1974) and the Security Council (Resolution 365/1974).

The Consequences of the Turkish Invasion

The Turkish invasion brought about two unintended changes: (1) the collapse of the junta that had ruled Greece since 1967 and the restoration of democracy in Greece with the return of Constantine Karamanlis from his self-imposed exile in Paris. Karamanlis had been the Greek prime minister who negotiated the 1959 Zurich and London Agreements on Cyprus; and (2) the collapse of the short-lived junta that was set up in Nicosia during the coup and the restoration of democracy in Cyprus. The speaker of the House of Representatives, Glafkos Clerides, became acting president under the constitution until the late fall of 1974, when the elected president, Archbishop Makarios, returned to Nicosia. However, as subsequent events have clearly shown, Turkey's real intention in invading Cyprus was to implement the long-desired partition of the island and not to restore democracy in either Greece or Cyprus. The Turkish invasion and occupation of 36.2 percent of the Republic of Cyprus radically changed the nature of the question and had serious consequences on a full range of political, security, humanitarian, and economic issues, including:

- The expulsion of the Greek Cypriot population from their ancestral homes in the areas occupied by the Turkish Army. Initially, some 142,000 Greek Cypriots were expelled. An additional 20,000 Greek Cypriots who had stayed behind were also forced out within the first two years of the Turkish occupation. Today, only about 500 enclaved Greek Cypriots remain in the occupied Karpass Peninsula in north-eastern Cyprus. In 1975, under the threat of further Turkish military action, the Turkish Cypriots living in the free areas of the republic were forcibly moved to the occupied areas. As a result of these actions nearly 50 percent of the total population of Cyprus was uprooted. Since then, Turkey has systematically deprived the displaced Greek Cypriots of their right to return to their homes and properties. This has given rise to celebrated and precedent-setting cases in the European Court of Human Rights (see legal decisions below).

- The dislocation and disruption of the Cypriot economy. This was caused by the forced population movement and the Turkish occupation of the most economically productive region of Cyprus.

- The death of over 4,000 Greek Cypriot civilians and military. An additional 1,476 Greek Cypriots remain missing. Most of the missing were last seen by the International Red Cross and other observers in Turkish custody. The human toll is even more serious when considered as a percentage of the population of Cyprus. Turkey has consistently refused to account for the fate of the missing.

- The ghetoization and isolation of the Turkish Cypriots. Turkey rigidly controlled access to the occupied areas until April 2003. It introduced the inflated Turkish lira as the currency of the occupied areas and brought Turkish bureaucrats to manage the economy of the occupied areas. The myth of the isolation of the Turkish Cypriots has already been discussed.

- The colonization of occupied Cyprus. Ankara has systematically introduced Anatolian settlers to the occupied areas in an attempt to alter the demographic composition of Cyprus and the Turkish Cypriot community. Most of these settlers have been granted "citizenship" of the so-called "TRNC." At the time of this writing, the number of settlers is estimated to be 160,000, while fewer than 85,000 Turkish Cypriots out of an estimated 124,000 at the time of the invasion in 1974 remain in the occupied areas. The introduction of settlers violates the 1949 Geneva Convention that Turkey has also ratified. The settlers have created social and cultural tensions in the occupied areas. Coupled with the bad economic conditions in the occupied areas, the colonization has caused Turkish Cypriots to migrate to countries like Germany, the United Kingdom, and Australia. Independent observers such as Alfons Cuco and Jaako Laakso have documented the situation for the Parliamentary Assembly of the Council of Europe in 1992 and 2003, respectively. The issue of the settlers was a major cause of the 2004 Greek Cypriot rejection of the Annan plan.

- The stationing of 43,000 Turkish troops armed with American weapons. These troops can be easily reinforced from major Turkish bases located some forty miles to the north of Cyprus. These troop deployments present a clear and present danger to the Republic of Cyprus.

- The systematic destruction of the Greek Cypriot cultural heritage in the occupied areas. Towns and villages have been given Turkish names in violation of international conventions. Archaeological sites have been looted and others have been destroyed in the name of development. Looted antiquities have been sold in the international black market. Churches and cemeteries have been desecrated, plundered, damaged, or converted to other uses. (See legal decisions.) Innumerable religious artifacts, icons, and other treasures have been stolen and smuggled abroad and illegally sold to art dealers. It should be noted that Turkey is a signatory of UNESCO and other related international conventions on the protection of cultural property.[22]

- The unlawful exploitation of stolen Greek Cypriot properties in the occupied areas. The usurpation, misappropriation, and illegal exploitation of Greek Cypriot properties has serious legal and political implications. (See legal decisions.) It was also a major reason for the Greek Cypriot rejection of the Annan plan in 2004. These actions violate the European Convention and Cypriot law, prejudice the search for a political solution, and have serious effects on the natural environment of the occupied areas.

- The de facto partition of Cyprus. The forcible population movement gave Turkey the opportunity to consolidate its administration of the occupied areas through the creation of an ethnically cleansed political entity. The first was the so-called "Turkish Federated State of Cyprus" ("TFSC"). Its announcement on 13 February 1975 was denounced by Resolution 367 of the UN Security Council. Rauf Denktash, the self-styled leader of the "TFSC" along with his Turkish masters went a step further eight years later. On 14 November 1983, the Turkish Cypriot pseudo-state unilaterally declared its independence from the Republic of Cyprus and renamed itself as the "Turkish Republic of Northern Cyprus" ("TRNC"). Security Council Resolution 541 of 18 November 1983 unanimously condemned this action. The council called on all states not to recognize this secessionist entity and reaffirmed all earlier resolutions on Cyprus. Since then, this entity has been recognized only by Turkey, which maintains that there are "two states and two peoples" on the island. Turkey insists that the new reality created on Cyprus in 1974 must be the foundation of any settlement of the Cyprus Question.

Legal Decisions on the Cyprus Question

A small, weak, and injured state, Cyprus has emphasized the rule of law in its attempt to secure its independence, sovereignty, and territorial integrity. During the Cold War, legal arguments had additional political significance as the members of the Western alliance claimed that the rule of law differentiated their behavior from that of the Eastern bloc. In the post-Cold War period, the rule of law was one of the characteristics of the much heralded "new world order."

The summaries of the legal decisions that follow provide an important independent record of how regional and national courts in Western Europe and the United States addressed the consequences of the Turkish invasion.[23] These decisions also have important political implications for any future settlement of the Cyprus Question. While affirming the legitimacy and continuity of the Republic of Cyprus and its government, these decisions have also found the Turkish Cypriot authorities to be nothing more than a "subordinate local administration" to that of Turkey. The findings of these precedent-setting decisions, especially on property issues, constitute an important foundation for any future comprehensive settlement of the Cyprus Question, especially in the aftermath of the accession of Cyprus to the EU. Turkey cannot continue to violate European law and court decisions and expect to make progress in its EU accession negotiations. The strength of the Cypriot legal position is such that it has influenced the content of resolutions adopted by the Security Council and General Assembly of the United Nations and other international organizations, shaped decisions of international and national courts, and contributed to the arms embargo imposed by the U.S. Congress on Turkey from 1974 to 1978.[24]

Following are some of the more representative and precedent-setting cases from the period from 1976 to 2005:

- *Cyprus v. Turkey* (6780/74) and (6950/75)—European Commission of Human Rights, 1976. In a joint report (1976) under former article 31 of the European Convention, Turkey was found to have violated articles 2 (right to life), 5 (liberty and security of the person), 8 (respect for private and family life, home, etc.), and 13 (effective remedies for violations of rights and freedoms), and article 1 of Protocol 1 (peaceful enjoyment of possessions). On 20 January 1979, the Committee of Ministers adopted resolution DH (79) calling for the enduring protection of human rights through intercommunal talks leading to a solution to the dispute.

- *Cyprus v. Turkey* (8007/77)—European Commission of Human Rights, 1983. Under former article 31 of the European Convention, the commission found Turkey in breach of its obligations under article 5 (liberty and security of the person) and article 8 (respect for private and family life, home, etc.), and article 1 of Protocol 1 (peaceful enjoyment of possessions). On 2 April 1992 the Committee of Ministers adopted resolution DH (92)12 in respect to the commission's report and made the 1983 report public.

- *Autocephalous Greek Orthodox Church of Cyprus v. Goldberg-Feldman Fine Arts Inc.*, 917 F.2d 278, U.S. Court of Appeals for the Seventh Circuit, decision of 24 October 1990. The U.S. Federal Circuit Court of Appeals affirmed the verdict of 3 August 1989 of the U.S. District Court in Indianapolis. The case involved the ownership of plundered sixth-century mosaics from the Church of Kanakaria in occupied Cyprus. The mosaics had been removed by Turkish antiquities smugglers and sold to an American dealer for $1.2 million. The mosaics were returned to their legitimate owner, the Church of

Cyprus. This decision has set an important precedent in the United States for the protection of cultural property. Even though it ratified the 1954 and 1970 UNESCO Conventions on the protection of cultural property, Turkey has done little to stop the vandalism, destruction, and plunder of Greek Cypriot cultural property in the areas controlled by the Turkish Army.

- Court of Justice of the European Communities—Case C-439/92, 5 July 1994. The court ruled that only import and phytosanitary certificates issued by the competent authorities of the Republic of Cyprus could be accepted by European Community member states. The ruling acknowledged that the only Cypriot state recognized by the European Community was the Republic of Cyprus. Import and phytosanitary certificates issued by Turkish Cypriot "authorities" were excluded because the "entity such as that established in the northern part of Cyprus . . . is recognized neither by the Community nor by the member states." The Court of Justice looked into the matter at the request of Britain's High Court following a case filed in the United Kingdom by Cypriot exporters of citrus fruit and potatoes. The High Court requested an interpretation of relevant provisions of the EC-Cyprus Association Agreement of 1972 and the EC Council Directive 77/93/EEC. Britain's High Court affirmed the Court of Justice decision in November 1994. This important decision recognized the sovereignty of the Republic of Cyprus over the whole of the island with regard to its relations with the European Community.
- *Loizidou v. Turkey*—European Court of Human Rights, 18 December 1996 and 28 July 1998. The European Court of Human Rights found that the applicant, Titina Loizidou, a citizen of the Republic of Cyprus, remained the legal owner of her property that was located in the areas occupied by the Turkish Army. The court made three judgments: on 23 March 1995 on preliminary objections, on 18 December 1996 on the merits of the case, and on 28 July 1998 on "just satisfaction." In a precedent-setting decision, the court regarded Turkey as an occupying power responsible for the policies and actions of the authorities in the occupied areas. These "authorities" were described as Turkey's "subordinate local administration." Turkey was found in breach of article 1, Protocol 1 of the Convention by its continuous denial to the plaintiff of access to her property and by its purported expropriation without compensation. On 28 July 1998, the court ordered Turkey to pay damages to Loizidou. Turkey's refusal to comply with the judgment resulted in resolutions by the Council of Ministers of the Council of Europe. These resolutions deplored Turkey's noncompliance, reminded Turkey of its acceptance of the Convention and of the court's compulsory jurisdiction, and called on the council to take appropriate steps to enforce compliance. With decisions pending on Turkey's EU application, in December 2003 Turkey paid the sum of Cyp£641,000, approximately $1.5 million, to Loizidou.

- *Cyprus v. Turkey* (Application No. 2581/94)—European Court of Human Rights, 10 May 2001. This is the most far-reaching decision on the applications filed by the government of the Republic of Cyprus against Turkey. The decision affirmed the earlier interstate applications by Cyprus under former article 31 of the Convention (10 July 1976 and 4 October 1983). The earlier cases had documented various violations of the Convention by Turkey during and since the 1974 invasion. By majority votes this decision determined that: (1) Turkey was in continuing violation of articles 2, 3, and 5 of the Convention by its failure to conduct effective investigations into the whereabouts and fate of the Greek Cypriot missing persons; (2) by its refusal to allow any Greek Cypriot displaced persons to return to their homes, Turkey was in continuing violation of article 8 of the Convention; similar continuing violations were found on article 1, Protocol 1 (denial of access, control, use, enjoyment of property rights) and article 13 (absence of effective remedies for the property rights of displaced Greek Cypriots); (3) Turkey violated the rights of Greek Cypriots living in "northern" Cyprus, including violations of article 9 (respectful treatment), article 10 (censorship of school books), article 1, Protocol 1 (peaceful enjoyment of possessions), article 2 (no appropriate secondary school facilities), article 3 (discrimination amounting to degrading treatment), and article 13 (absence of remedies); and (4) violations of Turkish Cypriot rights in the occupied areas under article 6 (trial of civilians by military courts). In addressing this case the court also affirmed the Loizidou case (1996 and 1998), the illegality of the proclamation of the "TRNC" in 1983 and of its "constitution" (1985), and the earlier decisions on the interstate applications filed by the Republic of Cyprus (6780/74, 6950/75, and 8007/77). The court held Turkey responsible for these violations as it had "effective overall control of northern Cyprus." The court also affirmed that the government of the Republic of Cyprus was the sole legitimate government on the island.
- *Admissibility Decision, Xenides-Arestis v. Turkey* (Application No. 46347/99)—European Court of Human Rights, 6 April 2005. In a unanimous decision, a chamber of the European Court of Human Rights declared admissible the application of Myra Xenides-Arestis. The applicant complained of a continuing violation of her rights under article 8 of the Convention (respect for home) and article 1, Protocol 1 (protection of property). Turkish military forces have deprived her of her right to property and home. The applicant also claimed that Turkey's actions constitute a violation of article 14 of the Convention (prohibition of discrimination). The applicant is Greek Cypriot and Greek Orthodox. Without prejudicing the merits of the case, the court rejected the presence of "domestic remedies" in the occupied areas. It also noted that because of the rejection of the UN plan (Annan-V) by the Greek Cypriots, its property provisions could not enter into force.

In conclusion, it should be noted that there are at least thirty-three additional major cases that have been declared admissible by the court.

Looking Back: How the Cold War Influenced the Cyprus Question

Chapters two and three examined the nature of the Cyprus Question, the reasons for the lack of a political settlement, the role of external actors in the search for a just and viable settlement of the question, and the changing role of the UN secretary-general. The fact remains that since 1975, negotiations for a solution to the Cyprus Question have been going on intermittently under UN auspices. The foundations for any functional and viable solution are four. They include: (1) the UN Security Council and General Assembly resolutions on Cyprus; (2) the 1977 and 1979 high-level agreements between Presidents Makarios and Kyprianou and Denktash; (3) European laws and conventions; and (4) the decisions of European and other national courts on the Cyprus case.

The 1977 and 1979 high-level agreements provided guidelines and a framework for negotiations to resolve the Cyprus Question. The goal was the establishment of an independent, bizonal federal republic whose government would have adequate powers to safeguard the unity, sovereignty, and territorial integrity of Cyprus. The agreements also emphasized respect for human rights and fundamental freedoms and gave priority to the return of Greek Cypriot displaced persons to Varosha, the modern city of Famagusta. Needless to say, none of these agreements have been honored or implemented by Turkey.

Until the early 1990s, Turkey relied on the Cold War concerns of the superpowers and on its strategic location to blunt international efforts for a just, lasting, and functional solution. In the post-Cold War period Turkey adapted its strategic importance to fit the new concerns of the United States and Europe. Turkey capitalized on the threat of regional instability in the Balkans and the Middle East, provided access to Central Asia's energy resources, and offered assistance in combating terrorism and Islamic fundamentalism. This is not the place to debate these assumptions. However, these assumptions played well in Washington and were reflected in continuing U.S. support for Turkey's positions on Cyprus.

The first major statement of Washington's Cyprus policy in the aftermath of the Turkish invasion came on 2 September 1975. Secretary of State Kissinger presented to the United Nations "five points" for the solution to the Cyprus Question. A settlement would protect the sovereignty, territorial integrity, and independence of Cyprus and provide territorial adjustments safeguarding the economic and security interests of the two communities and the autonomy of the Turkish Cypriots. These ideas found practical application in the Clifford Mission to Cyprus in February 1977. The U.S. presidential emissary convinced President Makarios to accept the principle of a bizonal federation as the basis for the solution to the Cyprus Question in return for the active engagement of the United States in the settlement process. These ideas became the foundation of detailed schemes presented through the United Nations since then and culminated in the five Annan plans presented between 2002 and 2004. It should be noted that there were no reciprocal concessions or commitments on the part of Turkey. Washington repeatedly relied on claims of upcoming negotiating initiatives to prevent sanctions on Turkey by

Congress or international and regional organizations and to water down the content of UN resolutions on Cyprus. Washington argued that this was necessary in order not to offend Turkey, encourage its negotiating flexibility, and assure its cooperation in U.S. regional strategy. Consequently, the burden of concessions fell on the weakest link, the victim of Turkey's aggression and its violations of American and international law.

Another aspect of American sensitivity toward Turkey's demands was in the pattern of negotiations proposed on Cyprus. The plan presented by the United States, Great Britain, and Canada on 10 November 1978 provides a good example.[25] The proposal required the agreement of Cyprus to a detailed constitutional framework creating a loose bicommunal, bizonal confederation as demanded by Turkey. However, issues of importance to the Greek Cypriots, such as the issue of territory, the return of the displaced to their ancestral homes, and withdrawal of the Turkish troops, were left open to future negotiations.

The deteriorating conditions in the Middle East with the fall of the shah of Iran, the Iran-Iraq War, and the Soviet invasion of Afghanistan strengthened Turkey's strategic significance in U.S. policy considerations. This was clearly understood by Turkey. With patience and persistence, Ankara promoted its partitionist schemes by capitalizing on Washington's regional security needs and influence in the United Nations.

CHAPTER SEVEN

Past Lessons

THIS BRIEF BOOK has given a bird's eye view of Cyprus and of the Cyprus Question. It has emphasized the contemporary aspects of the question, and provided a background of its evolution and how the involvement of external actors complicated and distorted it.

The Cyprus Question remains one of invasion and occupation. Cyprus, an EU member, remains the last divided and occupied country of Europe. This volume has called for a fresh approach to resolve the question based on the principles guiding the European Union, the unanimous UN Security Council resolutions, international and national court decisions, and the 1977 and 1979 high-level agreements. The continuing violations of human rights, massive colonization of areas under occupation, property usurpation, ethnic separation, destruction of cultural heritage, and continuing occupation and forcible division of Cyprus is an affront to the international legal order and a threat to regional stability.

As shown in this volume, on 1 May 2004 the Republic of Cyprus joined the European Union without achieving the desired goal of accession as a unified country. The government and people of Cyprus are committed to a just, functional, and viable settlement that would respect human rights and allow the peaceful reunification of their country in conformity with European norms. Chapter three showed in detail how and why the attempt to impose a settlement on Cyprus failed. The lessons of the 1999–2004 period must not be forgotten. Unfortunately, Ankara and its allies have attempted to use the positive Turkish Cypriot vote on Annan-V to attain the de facto recognition of Turkey's illegal creation. Such an action would consolidate division and enhance regional instability. It is in the interest of all involved in the Cyprus Question, particularly Turkey and the United States, to seek a settlement in conformity with EU norms and laws. While the pursuit of such a settlement does not replace the good offices of the United Nations, it provides the principles for a viable, functional, and just solution that will benefit both communities. At the time of this writing, Turkey, an applicant for EU accession, has yet to fulfill its obligations toward Cyprus. These obligations are part of the EU-Turkey accession document. Cyprus is now an EU issue and the implementation of EU rules cannot be avoided.

The Greek Cypriot commitment to the genuine reunification of Cyprus with the active contribution of the EU was highlighted in the address of the president of the Republic of Cyprus, Tassos Papadopoulos, on 18 September 2005 at the Sixtieth Session of the UN General Assembly. Turkey, under pressure from EU members, on 20 January 2006 presented a ten-point proposal for the resolution of the Cyprus Question. Unfortunately, this purported "new proposal" consisted of a repetition of Turkey's known positions on Cyprus. It was also an attempt by Turkey to void its obligations toward the EU and to upgrade the status of the secessionist entity it created in the occupied areas. The government of Cyprus rejected the Turkish proposal, while the United States and some EU members sought diplomatic ways not to close the door to further Turkish proposals.

Following behind-the-scenes negotiations, President Papadopoulos met with Secretary-General Kofi Annan in Paris on 28 February 2006. In a constructive exchange free from the recriminations heard in the aftermath of the referenda on "Annan-V," the two leaders reviewed the situation on Cyprus and examined modalities for moving forward on the reunification process. The carefully scripted press conference that followed the meeting and the statement read to the press was significant for both its symbolism and its content. The press conference took place in front of the flags of the United Nations and of the Republic of Cyprus. President Papadopoulos was appropriately referred to with his official title, while Talat was correctly mentioned as the leader of the Turkish Cypriot community. During the Annan negotiations from 1999 to 2004 there were only references to the "two leaders," while state symbols were notably absent. There were no references to the failed Annan plan, while Turkey's January proposals were not on the agenda for discussion. Instead, Turkey was reminded of its obligations toward Cyprus in the EU accession process and of the importance of reopening the city and port of Famagusta as a step in the settlement process. The UN Representative on Cyprus, Michael Moller, would work with the president of the republic and with the Turkish Cypriot leadership to reactivate the work of the Committee on the Missing Persons. He was also to help set up technical committees to discuss a series of issues in order to restore trust between the two communities and pave the way for the full resumption of negotiations. While the secretary-general noted that he had received assurances from the leader of the Turkish Cypriot community on the process outlined in the communiqué, Turkey and the Turkish Cypriots have disputed his statement. At the time of this writing neither Turkey nor its Turkish Cypriot surrogates appear to be willing to cooperate with the United Nations.

On 27 February 2006, the European Union with the consent of the Republic of Cyprus took an important step in extending a $165 million aid package for the development of the occupied areas. This became possible once the aid provision was separated from the proposed trade regulations for the occupied areas. Until then, Turkey and the Turkish Cypriots, with British support, had insisted on linking the two provisions in an attempt to gain the de facto recognition of the occupied areas. The result of this attempt was the loss of the first year's aid package. The aid was intended to promote harmonization with EU policy and support fields like energy and the environment in the occupied areas.

The accession of Cyprus to the EU and Turkey's application for EU accession provide new opportunities for the resolution of the Cyprus Question. While the government of the Republic of Cyprus and the Greek Cypriots have shown their commitment to the true reunification of their country, this has not been the case with Turkey or its surrogate Turkish Cypriot leadership in the occupied areas. Now the ball is in Turkey's court.

Much ink has been shed in describing the Cyprus Question. This protracted conflict has lasted too long, but for the first time in several decades a ray of hope exists. Without idealizing the European solution, the principles on which the EU is founded provide new venues for resolving issues that led to tragedy for all Cypriots, Greek and Turkish. We need to move beyond the fatalistic acceptance of this tragedy that has been justified in the name of political realism. We can and we must.

POSTSCRIPT

THIS MANUSCRIPT was submitted to the editor early in the spring of 2006. Since then, the following developments have occurred that may be of interest to the reader. Even though these developments are encouraging, Turkey and the Turkish Cypriot leadership have not moved beyond the positions analyzed in this volume.

On 28 February 2006, Cypriot President Tassos Papadopoulos met with UN Secretary-General Kofi Annan in Paris "to review the situation in Cyprus and examine modalities for moving forward on the process leading to the reunification of the island." They agreed that the resumption of negotiations within the framework of the secretary-general's good offices must be timely and based on careful preparation. The secretary-general was pleased to note that the leaders of both communities on Cyprus had already agreed that bicommunal discussions on a series of issues, agreement on which is necessary for the benefit of all Cypriots, would be undertaken at the technical level. Their agreement "to continue their ongoing dialogue with the expressed aim at accelerating the search for a comprehensive, fair and mutually acceptable solution to the Cyprus problem" generated a new momentum for the resumption of the Cyprus peace process.

At a UN-sponsored meeting on 8 July, President Papadopoulos and Turkish Cypriot leader Mehmet Ali Talat agreed on a set of principles, and also that "technical committees" on the Cyprus question should begin work at the end of July, while the leaders themselves would meet on occasion to review the process.

APPENDIX ONE

Resolution 186 (1964)
4 March 1964

The Security Council,
Noting that the present situation with regard to Cyprus is likely to threaten international peace and security and may further deteriorate unless additional measures are promptly taken to maintain peace and to seek out a durable solution,
Considering the positions taken by the parties in relation to the Treaties signed at Nicosia on 16 August 1960,
Having in mind the relevant provisions of the Charter of the United Nations and, in particular, its Article 2, paragraph 4, which reads:

"All Members shall refrain in their international relations from the threat or use of force against the territorial integrity or political independence of any State, or in any other manner inconsistent with the Purposes of the United Nations",

1. *Calls upon* all Member States, in conformity with their obligations under the Charter of the United Nations, to refrain from any action or threat of action likely to worsen the situation in the sovereign Republic of Cyprus, or to endanger international peace;
2. *Asks* the Government of Cyprus, which has the responsibility for the maintenance and restoration of law and order, to take all additional measures necessary to stop violence and bloodshed in Cyprus;
3. *Calls upon* the communities in Cyprus and their leaders to act with the utmost restraint;
4. *Recommends* the creation, with the consent of the Government of Cyprus, of a United Nations Peace-keeping Force in Cyprus. The composition and size of the Force shall be established by the Secretary-General, in consultation with the Governments of Cyprus, Greece, Turkey and the United Kingdom of Great Britain and Northern Ireland. The Commander of the Force shall be appointed by the Secretary-General and report to him. The Secretary-General, who shall keep the Governments providing the Force fully informed, shall report periodically to the Security Council on its operation;
5. *Recommends* that the function of the Force should be, in the interest of preserving international peace and security, to use its best efforts to prevent a

recurrence of fighting and, as necessary, to contribute to the maintenance and restoration of law and order and a return to normal conditions;

6. *Recommends* that the stationing of the Force shall be for a period of three months, all costs pertaining to it being met, in a manner to be agreed upon by them, by the Governments providing the contingents and by the Government of Cyprus. The Secretary-General may also accept voluntary contributions for that purpose;

7. *Recommends further* that the Secretary-General designate, in agreement with the Government of Cyprus and the Governments of Greece, Turkey and the United Kingdom, a mediator, who shall use his best endeavours with the representatives of the communities and also with the aforesaid four Governments, for the purpose of promoting a peaceful solution and an agreed settlement of the problem confronting Cyprus, in accordance with the Charter of the United Nations, having in mind the well-being of the people of Cyprus as a whole and the preservation of international peace and security. The mediator shall report periodically to the Secretary-General on his efforts;

8. *Requests* the Secretary-General to provide, from funds of the United Nations, as appropriate, for the remuneration and expenses of the mediator and his staff.

Adopted unanimously at the 1102nd meeting.

Resolution 187 (1964)
13 March 1964

The Security Council,
Having heard the statements of the representatives of the Republic of Cyprus, Greece and Turkey,
Reaffirming its resolution 186 (1964) of 4 March 1964,
Being deeply concerned over developments in the area,
Noting the progress reported by the Secretary-General in regard to the establishment of a United Nations Peace-keeping Force in Cyprus,
Noting the assurance from the Secretary-General that the United Nations Peace-keeping Force in Cyprus envisaged in resolution 186 (1964) is about to be established and that advance elements of that Force are already *en route* to Cyprus,

1. *Reaffirms* its call upon all Members States, in conformity with their obligations under the Charter of the United Nations, to refrain from any action or threat of action likely to worsen the situation in the sovereign Republic of Cyprus, or to endanger international peace;

2. *Requests* the Secretary-General to press on with his efforts to implement Security Council resolution 186 (1964), and requests Member States to co-operate with the Secretary-General to that end.

Adopted unanimously at the 1103rd meeting.

Resolution 353 (1974)
20 July 1974

The Security Council,
Having considered the report of the Secretary-General, at its 1779th meeting, about the recent developments in Cyprus,
Having heard the statement made of the President of the Republic of Cyprus and the statements of the representatives of Cyprus, Turkey, Greece and other Member States,
Having considered at its present meeting further developments in the island,
Deeply deploring the outbreak of violence and the continuing bloodshed,
Gravely concerned about the situation which has led to a serious threat to international peace and security, and which has created a most explosive situation in the whole Eastern Mediterranean area,
Equally concerned about the necessity to restore the constitutional structure of the Republic of Cyprus, established and guaranteed by international agreement,
Recalling its resolution 186 (1964) of 4 March 1964 and its subsequent resolutions on this matter,
Conscious of its primary responsibility for the maintenance of international peace and security in accordance with Article 24 of the Charter of the United Nations,
1. *Calls upon* all States to respect the sovereignty, independence and territorial integrity of Cyprus;
2. *Calls upon* all parties to the present fighting as a first step to cease all firing and requests all States to exercise the utmost restraint and to refrain from any action which might further aggravate the situation;
3. *Demands* an immediate end to foreign military intervention in the Republic of Cyprus that is in contravention of the provisions of paragraph 1 above;
4. *Requests* the withdrawal without delay from the Republic of Cyprus of foreign military personnel present otherwise than under the authority of international agreements, including those whose withdrawal was requested by the President of the Republic of Cyprus, Archbishop Makarios, in his letter of 2 July 1974;
5. *Calls upon* Greece, Turkey and the United Kingdom of Great Britain and Northern Ireland to enter into negotiations without delay for the restoration of peace in the area and constitutional government in Cyprus and to keep the Secretary-General informed;
6. *Calls upon* all parties to co-operate fully with the United Nations Peace-keeping Force in Cyprus to enable it to carry out its mandate;
7. *Decides* to keep the situation under constant review and asks the Secretary-General to report as appropriate with a view to adopting further measures in order to ensure that peaceful conditions are restored as soon as possible.
Adopted unanimously at the 1781st meeting.

Resolution 354 (1974)
23 July 1974

The Security Council,
Reaffirming the provisions of its resolution 353 (1974) of 20 July 1974,
Demands that all parties to the present fighting comply immediately with the provisions of paragraph 2 of Security Council resolution 353 (1974) calling for an immediate cessation of all firing in the area and requesting all States to exercise the utmost restraint and to refrain from any action which might further aggravate the situation.

Adopted unanimously at the 1783rd meeting.

Resolution 355 (1974)
1 August 1974

The Security Council,
Recalling its resolutions 186 (1964) of 4 March 1964, 353 (1974) of 20 July and 354 (1974) of 23 July 1974,
Noting that all States have declared their respect for the sovereignty, independence and territorial integrity of Cyprus,
Taking note of the Secretary-General's statement made at the 1788th meeting of the Security Council,
Requests the Secretary-General to take appropriate action in the light of his statement and to present a full report to the Council, taking into account that the cease-fire will be the first step in the full implementation of Security Council resolution 353 (1974).

Adopted at the 1789th meeting by 12 votes to none, with 2 abstentions (Byelorussian Soviet Socialist Republic, Union of Soviet Socialist Republics).

Resolution 358 (1974)
15 August 1974

The Security Council,
Deeply concerned about the continuation of violence and bloodshed in Cyprus,
Deeply deploring the non-compliance with its resolution 357 (1974) of 14 August 1974,
1. *Recalls* its resolutions 353 (1974) of 20 July, 354 (1974) of 23 July, 355 (1974) of 1 August 1974 and 357 (1974);
2. *Insists* on the full implementation of the above resolutions by all parties and on the immediate and strict observance of the cease-fire.

Adopted unanimously at the 1793rd meeting.

Resolution 360 (1974)
16 August 1974

The Security Council,
Recalling its resolutions 353 (1974) of 20 July, 354 (1974) of 23 July, 355 (1974) of 1 August, 357 (1974) of 14 August and 358 (1974) of 15 August 1974,
Noting that all States have declared their respect for the sovereignty, independence and territorial integrity of the Republic of Cyprus,
Gravely concerned at the deterioration of the situation in Cyprus, resulting from the further military operations, which constituted a most serious threat to peace and security in the Eastern Mediterranean area,
1. *Records its formal disapproval* of the unilateral military actions undertaken against the Republic of Cyprus;
2. *Urges* the parties to comply with all the provisions of previous resolutions of the Security Council, including those concerning the withdrawal without delay from the Republic of Cyprus of foreign military personnel present otherwise than under the authority of international agreements;
3. *Urges* the parties to resume without delay, in an atmosphere of constructive co-operation, the negotiations called for in resolution 353 (1974) whose outcome should not be impeded or prejudged by the acquisition of advantages resulting from military operations;
4. *Requests* the Secretary-General to report to the Council, as necessary, with a view to the possible adoption of further measures designed to promote the restoration of peaceful conditions;
5. *Decides* to remain seized of the question permanently and to meet at any time to consider measures which may be required in the light of the developing situation.
   Adopted at the 1794th meeting by 11 votes to none with 3 abstentions (Byelo-
      russian Soviet Socialist Republic, Iraq, Union of Soviet Socialist Republics).

Resolution 364 (1974)
13 December 1974

The Security Council,
Noting from the report of the Secretary-General of 6 December 1974 (S/11568), that in existing circumstances the presence of the United Nations Peace-keeping Force in Cyprus is still needed to perform the tasks it is currently undertaking if the cease-fire is to be maintained in the island and the search for a peaceful settlement facilitated,
Noting from the report the conditions prevailing in the island,
Noting also the statement by the Secretary-General contained in paragraph 81 of his report, that the parties concerned had signified their concurrence in his recommendation that the Security Council extend the stationing of the Force in Cyprus for a further period of six months,

Noting that the Government of Cyprus has agreed that in view of the prevailing conditions in the island it is necessary to keep the Force in Cyprus beyond 15 December 1974,

Noting also the letter dated 7 November 1974 (S/11557) from the Secretary-General to the President of the Security Council together with the text of resolution 3212 (XXIX) entitled "Question of Cyprus" adopted unanimously by the General Assembly at its 2275th plenary meeting on 1 November 1974,

Noting further that resolution 3212 (XXIX) enunciates certain principles intended to facilitate a solution to the current problems of Cyprus by peaceful means, in accordance with the purposes and principles of the United Nations,

1. *Reaffirms* its resolutions 186 (1964) of 4 March, 187 (1964) of 13 March, 192 (1964) of 20 June, 193 (1964) of 9 August, 194 (1964) of 25 September and 198 (1964) of 18 December 1964, 201 (1965) of 19 March, 206 (1965) of 15 June, 207 (1965) of 10 August and 219 (1965) of 17 December 1965, 220 (1966) of 16 March, 222 (1966) of 16 June and 231 (1966) of 15 December 1966, 238 (1967) of 19 June and 244 (1967) of 22 December 1967, 247 (1968) of 18 March, 254 (1968) of 18 June and 261 (1968) of 10 December 1968, 266 (1969) of 10 June and 274 (1969) of 11 December 1969, 281 (1970) of 9 June and 291 (1970) of 10 December 1970, 293 (1971) of 26 May and 305 (1971) of 13 December 1971, 315 (1972) of 15 June and 324 (1972) of 12 December 1972, 334 (1973) of 15 June and 343 (1973) of 14 December 1973 and 349 (1974) of 29 May 1974, and the consensus expressed by the President at the 1143rd meeting on 11 August 1964 and at the 1383rd meeting on 25 November 1967;

2. *Reaffirms* also its resolutions 353 (1974) of 20 July, 354 (1974) of 23 July, 355 (1974) of 1 August, 357 (1974) of 14 August, 358 (1974) and 359 (1974) of 15 August, 360 (1974) of 16 August and 361 (1974) of 30 August 1974;

3. *Urges* the parties concerned to act with the utmost restraint and to continue and accelerate determined co-operative efforts to achieve the objectives of the Security Council;

4. *Extends* once more the stationing in Cyprus of the United Nations Peace-keeping Force, established under Security Council resolution 186 (1964), for a further period ending 15 June 1975, in the expectation that by then sufficient progress towards a final solution will make possible a withdrawal or substantial reduction of the Force;

5. *Appeals again* to all parties concerned to extend their full co-operation to the United Nations Force in its continuing performance of its duties.

Adopted at the 1810th meeting by 14 votes to none.

Resolution 541 (1983)
18 November 1983

The Security Council,
Having heard the statement of the Foreign Minister of the Government of the Republic of Cyprus,

Concerned at the declaration by the Turkish Cypriot authorities issued on 15 November 1983 which purports to create an independent state in northern Cyprus,

Considering that this declaration is incompatible with the 1960 Treaty concerning the establishment of the Republic of Cyprus and the 1960 Treaty of Guarantee,

Considering, therefore, that the attempt to create a "Turkish Republic of Northern Cyprus" is invalid, and will contribute to a worsening of the situation in Cyprus,

Reaffirming its resolutions 365 (1974) and 367 (1975),

Aware of the need for a solution of the Cyprus problem based on the mission of good offices undertaken by the Secretary-General,

Affirming its continuing support for the United Nations Peace-keeping Force in Cyprus,

Taking note of the Secretary-General's statement of 17 November 1983,

1. *Deplores* the declaration of the Turkish Cypriot authorities of the purported secession of part of the Republic of Cyprus;

2. *Considers* the declaration referred to above as legally invalid and calls for its withdrawal;

3. *Calls for* the urgent and effective implementation of its resolutions 365 (1974) and 367 (1975);

4. *Requests* the Secretary-General to pursue his mission of good offices, in order to achieve the earliest possible progress towards a just and lasting settlement in Cyprus;

5. *Calls upon* the parties to co-operate fully with the Secretary-General in his mission of good offices;

6. *Calls upon* all States to respect the sovereignty, independence, territorial integrity and non-alignment of the Republic of Cyprus;

7. *Calls upon* all States not to recognise any Cypriot State other than the Republic of Cyprus;

8. *Calls upon* all States and the two communities in Cyprus to refrain from any action which might exacerbate the situation;

9. *Requests* the Secretary-General to keep the Security Council fully informed.

> *Adopted at the 2500th meeting by 13 votes to 1 against (Pakistan), with 1 abstention (Jordan).*

Resolution 550 (1984)
11 May 1984

The Security Council,

Having considered the situation in Cyprus at the request of the Government of the Republic of Cyprus,

Having heard the statement made by the President of the Republic of Cyprus,

Taking note of the report of the Secretary-General,

Recalling its resolutions 365 (1974), 367 (1975), 541 (1983) and 544 (1983),

Deeply regretting the non-implementation of its resolutions, in particular resolution 541 (1983),

Gravely concerned about the further secessionist acts in the occupied part of the Republic of Cyprus which are in violation of resolution 541 (1983), namely, the purported exchange of ambassadors between Turkey and the legally invalid "Turkish Republic of Northern Cyprus" and the contemplated holding of a "constitutional referendum" and "elections", as well as by other actions or threats of actions aimed at further consolidating the purported independent State and the division of Cyprus,

Deeply concerned about recent threats for settlement of Varosha by people other than its inhabitants,

Reaffirming its continuing support for the United Nations Peace-keeping Force in Cyprus,

1. *Reaffirms* its resolution 541 (1983) and calls for its urgent and effective implementation;

2. *Condemns* all secessionist actions, including the purported exchange of ambassadors between Turkey and the Turkish Cypriot leadership, declares them illegal and invalid and calls for their immediate withdrawal;

3. *Reiterates* the call upon all States not to recognize the purported State of the "Turkish Republic of Northern Cyprus" set up by secessionist acts and calls upon them not to facilitate or in any way assist the aforesaid secessionist entity;

4. *Calls upon* all States to respect the sovereignty, independence, territorial integrity, unity and non-alignment of the Republic of Cyprus;

5. *Considers* attempts to settle any part of Varosha by people other than its inhabitants as inadmissible and calls for the transfer of that area to the administration of the United Nations;

6. *Considers* any attempts to interfere with the status or the deployment of the United Nations Peace-keeping Force in Cyprus as contrary to the resolutions of the United Nations;

7. *Requests* the Secretary-General to promote the urgent implementation of Security Council resolution 541 (1983);

8. *Reaffirms* the mandate of good offices given to the Secretary-General and requests him to undertake new efforts to attain an overall solution to the Cyprus problem in conformity with the principles of the Charter of the United Nations and the provisions for such a settlement laid down in the pertinent United Nations resolutions, including resolution 541 (1983) and the present resolution;

9. *Calls upon* all parties to co-operate with the Secretary-General in his mission of good offices;

10. *Decides* to remain seized of the situation with a view to taking urgent and appropriate measures, in the event of non-implementation of resolution 541 (1983) and the present resolution;

11. *Requests* the Secretary-General to promote the implementation of the present resolution and to report thereon to the Security Council as developments require.

Adopted at the 2539th meeting by 13 votes to 1 (Pakistan), with 1 abstention (United States of America).

Resolution 3212 (XXIX)
1 November 1974

The General Assembly,
Having considered the question of Cyprus,
Gravely concerned about the continuation of the Cyprus crisis, which constitutes a threat to international peace and security,
Mindful of the need to solve this crisis without delay by peaceful means, in accordance with the purposes and principles of the United Nations,
Having heard the statements in the debate and taking note of the Report of the Special Political Committee on the question of Cyprus,
1. *Calls upon* all States to respect the sovereignty, independence, territorial integrity and non-alignment of the Republic of Cyprus and to refrain from all acts and interventions directed against it;
2. *Urges* the speedy withdrawal of all foreign armed forces and foreign military presence and personnel from the Republic of Cyprus, and the cessation of all foreign interference in its affairs;
3. *Considers* that the constitutional system of the Republic of Cyprus concerns the Greek-Cypriot and Turkish-Cypriot communities;
4. *Commends* the contacts and negotiations taking place on an equal footing, with the good offices of the Secretary-General, between the representatives of the two communities, and calls for their continuation with a view to reaching freely a mutually acceptable political settlement, based on their fundamental and legitimate rights;
5. *Considers* that all the refugees should return to their homes in safety and calls upon the parties concerned to undertake urgent measures to that end;
6. *Expresses the hope* that, if necessary, further efforts including negotiations can take place, within the framework of the United Nations, for the purpose of implementing the provisions of the present resolution, thus ensuring to the Republic of Cyprus its fundamental right to independence, sovereignty and territorial integrity;
7. *Requests* the Secretary-General to continue to provide United Nations humanitarian assistance to all parts of the population of Cyprus and calls upon all States to contribute to that effort;
8. *Calls upon* all parties to continue to co-operate fully with the United Nations Peace-keeping Force in Cyprus, which may be strengthened if necessary;
9. *Requests* the Secretary-General to continue to lend his good offices to the parties concerned;
10. *Further requests* the Secretary-General to bring the present resolution to the attention of the Security Council.

2275th plenary meeting
1 November 1974

Resolution 3395 (XXX)
20 November 1975

The General Assembly,
Having considered the question of Cyprus,
Having heard the statements in the debate and taking note of the Report of the Special Political Committee,
Noting with concern that four rounds of talks between the representatives of the two communities in pursuance of Security Council resolution 367 (1975) of 12 March 1975 have not yet led to a mutually acceptable settlement,
Deeply concerned at the continuation of the crisis in Cyprus,
Mindful of the need to solve the Cyprus crisis without further delay by peaceful means in accordance with the purposes and principles of the United Nations,
1. *Reaffirms* the urgent need for continued efforts for the effective implementation in all parts of General Assembly resolution 3212 (XXIX) of 1 November 1974 endorsed by the Security Council in its resolution 365 (1974) of 13 December 1974 and, to that end,
2. *Calls once again upon* all States to respect the sovereignty, independence, territorial integrity and non-alignment of the Republic of Cyprus and to refrain from all acts and interventions directed against it;
3. *Demands* the withdrawal without further delay of all foreign armed forces and foreign military presence and personnel from the Republic of Cyprus, and the cessation of all foreign interference in its affairs;
4. *Calls upon* the parties concerned to undertake urgent measures to facilitate the voluntary return of all refugees to their homes in safety and to settle all other aspects of the refugee problem;
5. *Calls* for the immediate resumption in a meaningful and constructive manner of the negotiations between the representatives of the two communities, under the auspices of the Secretary-General, to be conducted freely on an equal footing with a view to reaching a mutually acceptable agreement based on their fundamental and legitimate rights;
6. *Urges* all parties to refrain from unilateral action in contravention of resolution 3212 (XXIX), including changes in the demographic structure of Cyprus;
7. *Requests* the Secretary-General to continue his role in the negotiations between the representatives of the two communities;
8. *Also requests* the Secretary-General to bring the present resolution to the attention of the Security Council and to report on its implementation as soon as appropriate and not later than 31 March 1976;
9. *Calls upon* all parties to continue to co-operate fully with the United Nations Peace-keeping Force in Cyprus;
10. *Decides* to remain seized of this question.

2413th plenary meeting
20 November 1975

APPENDIX TWO

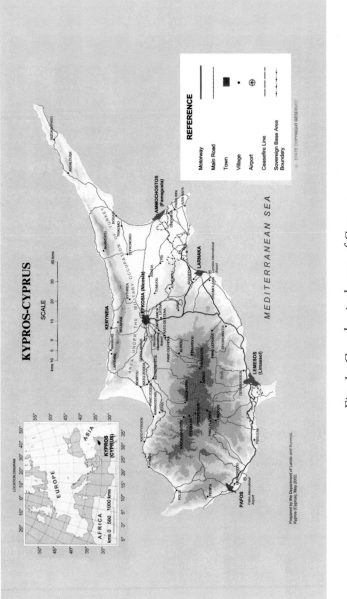

Fig. 1. *Geophysical map of Cyprus*
(Prepared by the Cyprus Department of Lands and Surveys)

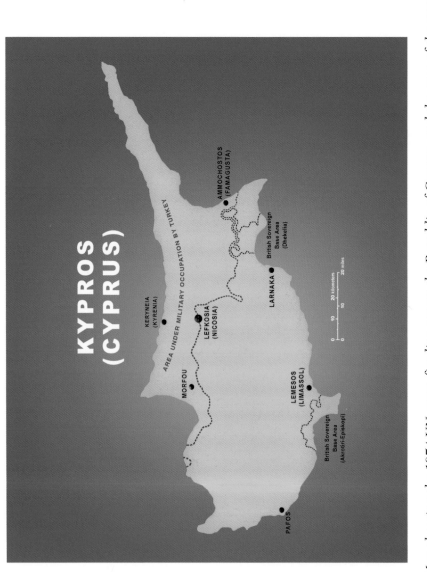

Fig. 2. Map showing the 1974 UN cease-fire line across the Republic of Cyprus, and the area of the republic under military occupation by Turkey

(Courtesy of the Press and Information Office, Republic of Cyprus)

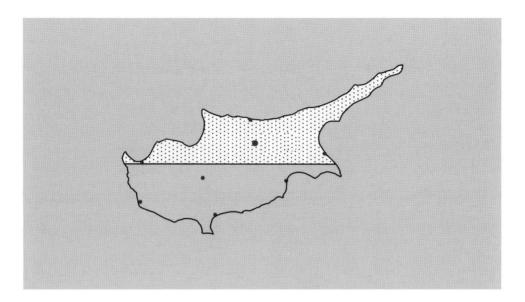

*Fig. 3. Partition of Cyprus as suggested in 1957 by Turkish Cypriot leader
Dr. Fazil Kutchuk in his pamphlet "The Cyprus Question: A Permanent
Solution," along the line shown on the map; the proposed "Turkish part" is the
shaded area in the north of the island
(Courtesy of the Press and Information Office, Republic of Cyprus)*

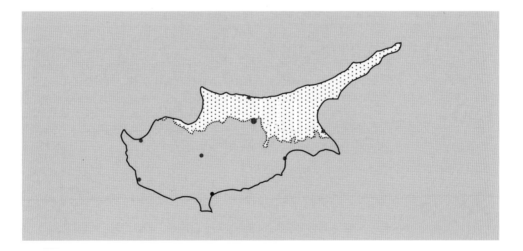

*Fig. 4. The dividing line as established by Turkey's invading army in 1974; the
shaded area in the north is still under military occupation by Turkey
(Courtesy of the Press and Information Office, Republic of Cyprus)*

Fig. 5. Map of the European Union that includes Cyprus
(Courtesy of the European Commission)

APPENDIX THREE

Statistical Information

Population

854,300 (December 2005)*
76.8 percent (652,200) Greek Cypriots**
10.3 percent (87,900) Turkish Cypriots
12.9 percent (110,200) foreign residents and workers
Population density: 88.4 persons per sq. km.

The population does not include the illegal settlers from Turkey (currently estimated at over 160,000) residing in the Turkish-occupied part of Cyprus.
**This figure includes the 8,000 (1 percent) Maronites, Armenians, and Latins who opted to join the Greek Cypriot community. Under the 1960 Constitution they had to choose to belong to either the Greek Cypriot or Turkish Cypriot community.*

Towns	Population (December 2005)
Nicosia (Lefkosia) (capital)	224,500*
Limassol (Lemesos)	176,900
Larnaca (Larnaka)	79,000
Paphos (Pafos)	52,800

The population in the Government-controlled part of the city only.

Towns under Turkey's occupation	Population*
Famagusta (Ammochostos)	38,960
Morphou (Morfou)	7,466
Kyrenia (Keryneia)	3,892

Population prior to 1974 Turkish invasion.

Vital Statistics

Birth rate	11.3 per thousand (2004)
Death rate	7.1 per thousand (2004)
Growth rate	2.1 percent (2005)
Life expectancy (males)	77.0 (2003)
Life expectancy (females)	81.4 (2003)

Other Economic Data (2005)

Per capita income	Cyp£10,383*
Inflation	2.6 percent
Rate of Growth	3.8 percent
Unemployment	3.7 percent
Economically active population	354,900
Gainfully employed	329,500

*U.S.$24,515.

NOTES

Chapter One

1.   Costas P. Kyrris, *History of Cyprus* (Nicosia: Lampousa Publications, 1996).

2.   See chapter six.

3.   See chapter four.

4.   P. Kitromilides and M. Evriviades, *Cyprus*, rev. ed. (Denver: Clio Press, 1995).

5.   J. Hackett, *A History of the Orthodox Church of Cyprus* (New York: Burt Franklin, 1972).

6.   G. S. Georgallides, *A Political and Administrative History of Cyprus 1918–1926* (Nicosia: Cyprus Research Centre, 1979); and idem, *Cyprus and the Governorship of Sir Ronald Storrs: The Causes of the 1931 Crisis* (Nicosia: Cyprus Research Centre, 1985).

7.   See legal cases, chapter six.

8.   See note 6 above.

9.   Robert Holland, *Britain and the Revolt in Cyprus, 1955–1959* (Oxford: Clarendon Press/Oxford, 1998).

10.   See chapter six.

11.   Van Coufoudakis, "Cyprus," in *Political Parties of Europe*, ed. Vincent E. McHale (Westport, Conn.: Greenwood Press, 1983), 104-34.

Chapter Two

1.   Republic of Cyprus, Press and Information Office, *Resolutions Adopted by the United Nations on the Cyprus Problem, 1964–2001* (Nicosia: PIO, 2002).

2.   See chapter six.

3.   European Commission, "Protocol Regarding the Adaptation of the Ankara Agreement to the Ten New Member States," press release, 29 March 2005.

4.   See note 1.

5.   United Nations Security Council, S/6253 (1965).

6.   Cmnd. 42 (London: HMSO, 1956); also, United Nations Security Council, S/6253 (1965).

7.   See legal cases, chapter six.

8.   Rapporteurs A. Cuco, 1992, and J. Laasko, 2003.

9.   See note 3.

10.   Republic of Cyprus, Ministry of Foreign Affairs, "Turkey's Persistent Vetoing of Cyprus' Membership in International Organizations, Arrangements and Treaties," press release, Nicosia, 11 November 2005.

Chapter Three

1.   See chapter five.

2.   Sir David Hannay, *Cyprus: The Search for a Solution* (London: I. B. Tauris, 2005).

3.   "Declaration on Regional Issues," press release, 20 June 1999, p. 3.

4.   See chapter six, Legal Cases.

5.   Alfred Moses at the American Hellenic Institute, Washington, D.C., 24 October 2000, American Hellenic Institute, Press Release 54/2000.

6.   The chapter on "The Pacific Settlement of Disputes."

7.   The text of the letter of invitation can be found in Claire Palley, *An International Relations Debacle: The UN Secretary-General's Mission of Good Offices in Cyprus 1999–2004* (Portland, Ore.: Hart Publishers, 2005), 346-51.

8.   Ibid., 5-12. Claire Palley, a well-known British constitutional authority, served as advisor to various governments of the Republic of Cyprus.

9.   See http://www.cyprus-un-plan.org/.

10.   "Cyprus: Bi-Communal Development Program Evaluation," 25 May 2004, submitted to the U.S. Agency for International Development by Development Associates Inc., of Arlington, Virginia, in collaboration with Nathan and Associates.

11.   Palley (*An International Relations Debacle*, 276-314) provides an excellent comparative summary of Annan I-V.

12.   See chapter six, Legal Cases.

Chapter Four

1.   Republic of Cyprus, Public Information Office, op. cit.

2.   See chapter six, Legal Cases.

3.   Embassy of Cyprus, "Contributions of the Republic of Cyprus to the Economic Development of Cypriots of Turkish Ethnic Origin," press release, Washington, D.C., 1 April 2005.

4.   See Michael Jansen, *War and Cultural Heritage: Cyprus after the 1974 Turkish Invasion,* Minnesota Mediterranean and East European Monographs, no. 14 (Minneapolis: University of Minnesota, Modern Greek Studies, 2005).

5.   European Commission, "Declaration by the European Union and its Member States in Response to the Declaration by Turkey made at the Time of Signature of the Additional Protocol to the Ankara Agreement," press release, 21 September 2005.

6.   European Commission, Brussels, 3 October 2005.

Chapter Five

1. For the text, see Republic of Cyprus, Public Information Office, *European Stand on the Cyprus Problem* (Nicosia: PIO, 2003), 66-68.

2. Ibid., 101-5.

3. Ibid., Conclusions of the Presidency, 157-59.

4. The legal and political criteria that include the rule of law, observance of human rights, democratic procedures, and economic issues such as a free market economy, etc.

5. "Widening": the expansion of the EU. "Deepening": the greater integration and cohesion of EU institutions and procedures.

6. Constantine Stefanou, ed., *Cyprus and the EU: The Road to Accession* (Burlington, Vt.: Ashgate Publishing Co., 2005).

7. Yannos Kranidiotis, the son of a well-known Cypriot diplomat, was killed in an airplane accident on 13 September 1999.

8. Republic of Cyprus, Press and Information Office, *European Stand*, 123-24.

9. Turkey argued that under the 1960 independence agreements Cyprus could not join any organizations that did not include Turkey.

10. Republic of Cyprus, Press and Information Office, *European Stand*, 159-60.

11. See Stefanou, ed., *Cyprus and the EU*.

12. The Imia crisis involved claims by Turkey over some uninhabited Greek islets in the Aegean Sea. Late in December 1995 and into early 1996 an incident involving rescue operations over a grounded Turkish cargo vessel created a near confrontation between the two countries. The conflict was averted by an American diplomatic intervention. The 1998 Ocalan incident involved the arrest of the Kurdish leader in a combined CIA/Turkish intelligence operation. Greece had been accused of facilitating Ocalan's run from the Turkish authorities.

13. See the summary of Talat's comments in a lecture given at the Brookings Institution in Washington, D.C., 26 October 2005; and "Turkish Cypriot Expectations from the EU," *Turkish Policy Quarterly* (fall 2005, online edition).

Chapter Six

1. With the help of key Turkish Cypriot leaders like Rauf Denktash, Turkey created, financed, trained, and equipped a Turkish Cypriot terrorist organization known as the TMT (Turkish Resistance Organization). This group included members of the Turkish special forces. The TMT's formation was announced in November 1957. The organization was the successor to Volkan, another similar terrorist group. Denktash has admitted his role and his many terrorist activities which were intended to create intercommunal tensions. See his interview on Britain's ITV, 26 June 1984.

2. The plan was named after the British prime minister. See Great Britain, *Cyprus: Statement of Policy*, Cmnd. 455 (London: HMSO, 1958).

Greece and the Greek Cypriots rejected the plan because it aimed at the partition of Cyprus.

3.   For the full texts of the independence agreements, see *Cyprus*, Cmnd. 1093 (London: HMSO, 1960). The more complete texts have been edited by Ambassador Nicolas D. Macris, *The 1960 Treaties on Cyprus and Selected Subsequent Acts* (Mannheim: Bibliopolis, 2003).

4.   Turkey argues that Cyprus cannot be a member of an international organization that does not include the guarantor powers. Turkey attempted to use this argument in the case of the Cypriot application for EU accession. Turkey's objection aimed at stopping the Cypriot application and/or linking the Cypriot application to Turkey's case. Turkey failed in both objectives. Further, a secret memo of understanding between Greece and Turkey called for measures to be taken to control communism in Cyprus.

5.   Thomas Ehrlich, "Cyprus the 'Warlike Isle': Origins and Elements of the Current Crisis," *Stanford Law Review* 18 (May 1966): 1021-98. See also S. A. de Smith, "Cyprus: Sui Generis," in *The New Commonwealth and its Constitutions* (London: Stevens and Sons, 1964), 282-96.

6.   "Analysis of the Cyprus Agreements," 14 July 1959.

7.   As in the case of the Greco-Turkish talks in 1965, 1967, and 1971.

8.   See page 82.

9.   George Ball considered replacing Makarios with General Grivas, a Makarios critic who led the military aspect of the anticolonial struggle.

10.   See Diana Weston Markides, *Cyprus 1957–1963, From Colonial Conflict to Constitutional Crisis: The Key Role of the Municipal Issue*, Minnesota Mediterranean and East European Monographs, no. 8 (Minneapolis: University of Minnesota, Modern Greek Studies, 2001).

11.   Brendan O'Malley and Ian Craig, *The Cyprus Conspiracy: America, Espionage and the Turkish Invasion* (London: I. B. Tauris and Co., Ltd., 1999).

12.   Statements made to the *New York Times* and the *New York Herald Tribune* on 31 December 1963.

13.   Jolyon Jenkins, "The UK's Murky Role in the Cyprus Crisis," BBC Radio 4 Document, 23 January 2006.

14.   Dean Acheson, "Cyprus: The Anatomy of the Problem," *Chicago Bar Record* 46, no. 8 (May 1965): 349-56. The text is Acheson's address to the Chicago Bar Association on 24 March 1965.

15.   United Nations Security Council, S/6253.

16.   A good account of the crisis is offered by U.S. ambassador to Turkey Parker T. Hart, *Two NATO Allies at the Threshold of War: Cyprus, A First Hand Account of Crisis Management 1965–1968* (Durham, S.C.: Duke University Press, 1990).

17.   Judge Michael Dekleris from Greece and Professor Orhan Aldikacti from Turkey.

18.   Both Justice Dekleris and Professor Aldikacti in interviews and documents in their possession confirm this agreement. See also Justice Dekleris's book, *Κυπριακό 1972–1974: Η Τελευταία Ευκαιρία* (Cyprus 1972–1974: The Last Opportunity) (Athens: published by the author, 1981).

19.   See the letter by Greek ambassador Angelos Chorafas of 18 June 1971 to President Makarios.

20.   As part of its independent foreign policy during the Cold War, Turkey turned a blind eye to the restrictions of the 1939 Montreux Treaty on the navigation of warships through the Straits. This helped greatly the composition of the Soviet Fifth Eskadra in the Mediterranean.

21.   Measures could have included the interposition of the Sixth Fleet between the invading force and Cyprus, the use of the U.S. Air Force to control the airspace around Cyprus, and the suspension of U.S. weapons sales and shipment of spare parts required by the Turkish forces.

22.   The most recent study on the subject is by journalist Michael Jansen, *War and Cultural Heritage*.

23.   The summary of the legal cases comes from the publication by the Republic of Cyprus, Press and Information Office, *The Cyprus Question: A Brief Introduction* (Nicosia: PIO, 2005), 23-26.

24.   Among the many studies on the subject, see Ian Brownlie, "The Prohibition of the Use of Armed Force for the Solution of International Differences with Particular Reference to the Affairs of the Republic of Cyprus," in *International Law Conference on Cyprus—1979* (Nicosia: Cyprus Bar Council, 1981), 198-226. See also Eugene T. Rossides, "Cyprus and the Rule of Law," *Syracuse Journal of International Law and Commerce* 17, no. 1 (spring 1991): 21-90.

25.   This came to be known as the "ABC" plan (i.e., American, British, Canadian plan) or the Nimetz Plan, after Matthew Nimetz, the American diplomat who presented the plan.

GLOSSARY

Acquis communautaire	the body of legislation guiding European Union policy
AKEL	Progressive Party of the Working People, the Communist Party of Cyprus
Annan plan	the comprehensive plan prepared by the staff of UN secretary-general Kofi Annan, along with American and British diplomats; five versions of the plan were presented between November 2002 and March 2004
CFSP	Common Foreign and Security Policy of the EU
COREPER	the EU Council's committee of permanent representatives
Enosis	the movement for the union of Cyprus with Greece
EMU	European Monetary Union
EPC	European Political Cooperation
EU	European Union; earlier, the EEC (European Economic Community)
FYROM	Former Yugoslav Republic of Macedonia; created from the break-up of Yugoslavia
G8	Group of Eight (G8) (Canada, France, Germany, Italy, Japan, Russia, the United Kingdom, and the United States); heads of government meet annually to discuss major economic and political policy issues
GATT	General Agreement on Tariffs and Trade, the precursor of the World Trade Organization (WTO)

Mission of Good Offices	services offered by the UN Secretariat to assist in conflict resolution
NGO	Nongovernmental organization
Non-paper	an informal document submitted in negotiations to test ideas; acceptance and discussion of these papers involves no commitments by the parties involved
PFP	Partnership for Peace
SBAs	Sovereign Base Areas; military bases Great Britain acquired on Cypriot soil with the 1960 independence agreements for Cyprus
Schengen Agreement	the EU agreement regulating access to the EU by non-EU nationals
TMT	Turk Mukavemet Teskilati (Turkish Resistance Organization); formed in 1957 by Rauf Denktash to counter Greek Cypriot demands for union with Greece
"TRNC"	"Turkish Republic of Northern Cyprus," declared in the occupied areas by the Turkish Army in November 1983 and recognized only by Turkey
UNFICYP	United Nations Force in Cyprus, the peacekeeping force created in March 1964 by UN Security Council Resolution 186
UNOPS	United Nations Office for Project Services in Nicosia
WTO	World Trade Organization

BIBLIOGRAPHY

This select bibliography reflects only sources in English. These sources are in addition to the endnote references in the text. There is a wealth of literature in other languages. For useful publications by the Press and Information Office of the Republic of Cyprus, please visit www.moi.gov.cy/pio.

Attalides, Michael. *Cyprus: Nationalism and International Politics.* Edinburgh: Q Press, 1979.

Averoff-Tossizza, Evangelos. *Lost Opportunities: The Cyprus Question 1950–1963.* New Rochelle, N.Y.: A. D. Caratzas, 1986.

Bank of Cyprus, Cultural Foundation. *Cyprus: 2500 Years of Cartography.* Nicosia: Bank of Cyprus, 1986.

Brownlie, Ian. "The Prohibition of the Use of Armed Force for the Solution of International Differences with Particular Reference to the Affairs of the Republic of Cyprus." In *International Law Conference on Cyprus: 1979*, 198-226. Nicosia: Cyprus Bar Council, 1981.

Christodoulou, Demetrios. *Inside the Cyprus Miracle: The Labours of an Embattled Mini-Economy.* Minnesota Mediterranean and East European Monographs, no. 2. Minneapolis: University of Minnesota, Modern Greek Studies, 1992.

Chrysostomides, Kypros. *The Republic of Cyprus: A Study in International Law.* The Hague: Martinus Nijhoff, 2000.

Clerides, Glafkos. *Η Κατάθεσή μου* (My deposition). 4 vols. Nicosia: Alithia Publishers, 1989–92.

———. "Reflections on the Cyprus Problem." *Modern Greek Studies Yearbook* 10/11 (1994/95): 1-6.

Copley, Gregory R. "Turkish Strategic Imperatives and Western Policy Failures Led to the Collapse of the Cyprus Resolution Talks." *Defense and Foreign Affairs Daily*, 24 June 2004.

Crawshaw, Nancy. *The Cyprus Revolt: An Account of the Struggle for Union with Greece.* London: George Allen and Unwin, 1978.

Denktash, Rauf R. *The Cyprus Triangle.* Nicosia: K. Rustem, 1982.

Ehrlich, Thomas. *Cyprus 1958–1967.* New York: Oxford University Press, 1974.

Emiliou, Nicholas. "The Prohibition of the Use of Force in International Law and the Cyprus Problem." *Modern Greek Studies Yearbook* 10/11 (1994/95): 171-203.

Foley, Charles. *Island in Revolt.* London: Longmans, 1962.

Gazioglu, Ahmet C. *The Turks in Cyprus: A Province of the Ottoman Empire (1571–1878)*. London: K. Rustem, 1990.

Georghallides, G. S. *A Political and Administrative History of Cyprus, 1918–1926, with a Survey of the Foundation of British Rule*. Nicosia: Cyprus Research Centre, 1979.

———. *Cyprus and the Governorship of Sir Ronald Storrs: The Causes of the 1931 Crisis*. Nicosia: Cyprus Research Centre, 1985.

Hatzivassiliou, Evanthis. *Britain and the International Status of Cyprus, 1955–59*. Minnesota Mediterranean and East European Monographs, no. 6. Minneapolis: University of Minnesota, Modern Greek Studies, 1997.

———. *The Cyprus Question, 1878–1960: The Constitutional Aspect*. Minnesota Mediterranean and East European Monographs, no. 11. Minneapolis: University of Minnesota, Modern Greek Studies, 2002.

Hill, Sir George. *A History of Cyprus*. 4 vols. Cambridge: Cambridge University Press, 1940–52.

Hitchens, Christopher. *Hostage to History: Cyprus from the Ottomans to Kissinger*. London: Verso, 1997.

Holland, Robert. *Britain and the Revolt in Cyprus*. Oxford: Clarendon Press, 1998.

Hunt, Sir David, ed. *Footprints in Cyprus: An Illustrated History*. London: Trigraph, 1982.

Ioannides, Christos P. *In Turkey's Image: The Transformation of Occupied Cyprus into a Turkish Province*. New Rochelle, N.Y.: A. D. Caratzas, 1991.

———. *Realpolitik in the Eastern Mediterranean: From Kissinger and the Cyprus Crisis to Carter and the Lifting of the Turkish Arms Embargo*. New York: Pella Pub. Co., 2001.

James, Alan. *Keeping the Peace in the Cyprus Crisis of 1963–1964*. New York: Palgrave, 1992.

Jansen, Michael. *War and Cultural Heritage: Cyprus after the 1974 Turkish Invasion*. Minnesota Mediterranean and East European Monographs, no. 14. Minneapolis: University of Minnesota, Modern Greek Studies, 2005.

Katsiaounis, Rolandos. *Labour, Society and Politics in Cyprus during the Second Half of the Nineteenth Century*. Nicosia: Cyprus Research Centre, 1996.

Kazamias, G. "Greece, Enosis, Anticommunism, and the Junta: Early Perceptions of the Colonels' Regime in Cyprus." *Modern Greek Studies Yearbook* 18/19 (2002/2003): 253-70.

Kitromilides, P., and M. Evriviades, comps. *Cyprus: A Bibliography*. Rev. ed. Denver, Colo.: Clio Press, 1995.

Kranidiotis, Yannos N. "Relations between Cyprus and the European Community." *Modern Greek Studies Yearbook* 8 (1992): 165-206.

Kyriakides, Stanley. *Cyprus: Constitutionalism and Crisis Government*. Philadelphia: University of Pennsylvania Press, 1968.

Kyrris, Costas P. *History of Cyprus*. Nicosia: Lampusa, 1996.

Luke, Sir Harry. *Cyprus under the Turks, 1571-1878: A Record Based on the Archives of the English Consulate in Cyprus under the Levant Company and After.* Oxford: Clarendon Press, 1921.

Papacosma, S. Victor, James Sperling, and Andreas Theophanous, eds. *EU Enlargement and New Security Challenges in the Eastern Mediterranean.* Nicosia: Intercollege Press, 2004.

Polyviou, Polyvios. *Cyprus, Conflict and Negotiation, 1960–1980.* London: Duckworth, 1980.

Rizas, Sotiris. "American and British Policy toward Cyprus, 1963–1964." *Modern Greek Studies Yearbook* 18/19 (2002/2003): 151-180.

———. "The Greek Military Regime's Policy towards Cyprus, 1967–1974." *Modern Greek Studies Yearbook* 18/19 (2002/2003): 239-52.

Salem, Norma, ed. *Cyprus: A Regional Conflict and Its Resolution.* New York: St. Martin's Press, in association with the Canadian Institute for International Peace and Security, Ottawa, 1992.

Scheffer, David J. "Human Rights and the New World Order: The Relevance of Cyprus." *Modern Greek Studies Yearbook* 8 (1992): 207-19.

Scherer, John. *Blocking the Sun: The Cyprus Conflict.* Minnesota Mediterranean and East European Monographs, no. 5. Minneapolis: University of Minnesota, Modern Greek Studies, 1997.

Stearns, Monteagle. *Entangled Allies: U.S. Policy toward Greece, Turkey, and Cyprus.* New York: Council on Foreign Relations, 1992.

Stegenga, James. *The United Nations Force in Cyprus.* Columbus: Ohio State University Press, 1968.

Stern, Laurence M. *The Wrong Horse: The Politics of Intervention and the Failure of American Diplomacy.* New York: Times Books, 1977.

Theophanous, Andreas. *The Cyprus Question and the EU: The Challenge and the Promise.* Nicosia: Intercollege Press, 2004.

Vassiliou, George. "Managing Ethnic Conflicts in the New World Order: The Case of Cyprus." *Modern Greek Studies Yearbook* 10/11 (1994/95): 7-16.

Windsor, Philip. *NATO and the Cyprus Crisis.* Adelphi Papers, no. 14. London, 1964.

Xydis, Stephen G. *Cyprus: Conflict and Conciliation, 1954–1958.* Columbus: Ohio State University Press, 1967.

———. *Cyprus: The Reluctant Republic.* The Hague: Mouton, 1973.

INDEX